ESSENTIALS OF FORENSIC SCIENCE

Science versus Crime

ESSENTIALS OF
FORENSIC SCIENCE

Science versus Crime

Max M. Houck

SET EDITOR
Suzanne Bell, Ph.D.

Facts On File
An imprint of Infobase Publishing

Facts On File, Inc.
An imprint of Infobase Publishing
132 West 31st Street
New York NY 10001

Library of Congress Cataloging-in-Publication Data
Houck, Max M.
    Science versus crime / by Max M. Houck.
        p. cm.—(Essentials of forensic science)
    Includes bibliographical references and index.
    ISBN-13: 978-0-8160-5508-1 (acid-free paper)
    ISBN-10: 0-8160-5508-4 (acid-free paper)
    1. Criminal investigation—United States 2. Forensic sciences—United States. 3. Evidence, Criminal—United States. I. Title.
    HV8073.H777 2009
    363.250973—dc22   2008003499

Facts On File books are available at special discounts when purchased in bulk quantities for businesses, associations, institutions, or sales promotions. Please call our Special Sales Department in New York at (212) 967-8800 or (800) 322-8755.

You can find Facts On File on the World Wide Web at http://www.factsonfile.com

Text design by Erik Lindstrom
Illustrations by Accurate Art, Inc.
Photo research by Suzanne M. Tibor, Ph.D.

Printed in the United States of America

MP ML 10 9 8 7 6 5 4 3 2 1

This book is printed on acid-free paper and contains 30 percent postconsumer recycled content.

This book is dedicated to Simon Lewis, for giving me my last chance.

CONTENTS

PREFACE

Forensic science has become in the early 21st century what the space race was in the 1960s—an accessible and inspiring window into the world of science. The surge in popularity that began in the latter part of the 20th century echoes a boom that began in the later part of the 19th century and was labeled the "Sherlock Holmes effect." Today it is called the "C.S.I. effect," but the consequences are the same as they were a century ago. The public has developed a seemingly insatiable appetite for anything forensic, be it fiction, reality, or somewhere between.

Essentials of Forensic Science is a set that is written in response to this thirst for knowledge and information. Written by eminent forensic scientists, the books cover the critical core of forensic science from its earliest inception to the modern laboratory and courtroom.

Forensic science is broadly defined as the application of science to legal matters, be they criminal cases or civil lawsuits. The history of the law dates back to the earliest civilizations, such as the Sumerians and the Egyptians, starting around 5000 B.C.E. The roots of science are older than civilization. Early humans understood how to make tools, how to cook food, how to distinguish between edible and inedible plants, and how to make rudimentary paints. This knowledge was technical and not based on any underlying unifying principles. The core of these behaviors is the drive to learn, which as a survival strategy was invaluable. Humans learned to cope with different environments and conditions, allowing adaptation when other organisms could not. Ironically, the information encoded in human DNA gives us the ability to analyze, classify, and type it.

Science as a formalized system of thinking can be traced to the ancient Greeks, who were the first to impose systematic patterns of thought and analysis to observations. This occurred around 500 B.C.E. The Greeks organized ideas about the natural world and were able to conceive of advanced concepts. They postulated the atom (from the

Greek word *atomos*) as the fundamental unit of all matter. The Greeks were also among the first to study anatomy, medicine, and physiology in a systematic way and to leave extensive written records of their work. They also formalized the concept of the autopsy.

From ancient roots to modern practice the history of forensic science winds through the Middle Ages, alchemy, and the fear of poisoning. In 1840 pivotal scientific testimony was given by Mathieu-Joseph-Bonaventure (Mateu Josep Bonaventura) Orfila (1787–1853) in a trial in Paris related to a suspected case of arsenic poisoning. His scientific technique and testimony marks the beginning of modern forensic science. Today the field is divided into specialties such as biology (DNA analysis), chemistry, firearms and tool marks, questioned documents, toxicology, and pathology. This division is less than a half-century old. In Orfila's time the first to practice forensic science were doctors, chemists, lawyers, investigators, biologists, and microscopists with other skills and interests that happened to be of use to the legal system. Their testimony was and remains opinion testimony, something the legal system was slow to embrace. Early courts trusted swearing by oath—better still if oaths of others supported it. Eyewitnesses were also valued, even if their motives were less than honorable. Only in the last century has the scientific expert been integrated into the legal arena with a meaningful role. Essentials of Forensic Science is a distillation of the short history and current status of modern forensic science.

The set is divided into seven volumes:

☑ *Science versus Crime* by Max Houck, director of research — forensic science, West Virginia University; Fellow, American Academy of Forensic Sciences; formerly of the FBI (trace evidence analyst/anthropologist), working at the Pentagon and Waco. This book covers the important cases and procedures that govern scientific evidence, the roles of testimony and admissibility hearings, and how the law and scientific evidence intersect in a courtroom.

☑ *Blood, Bugs, and Plants* by Dr. R. E. Gaensslen, professor, forensic science; head of program and director of graduate studies; Distinguished Fellow, American Academy of Forensic

Sciences; former editor of the *Journal of Forensic Sciences.* This book delves into the many facets of forensic biology. Topics include a historical review of forensic serology (ABO blood groups), DNA typing, forensic entomology, forensic ecology, and forensic botany.

☑ *Drugs, Poisons, and Chemistry* by Dr. Suzanne Bell, Bennett Department of Chemistry, West Virginia University; Fellow of the American Board of Criminalistics; and Fellow of the American Academy of Forensics. This book covers topics in forensic chemistry, including an overview of drugs and poisons, both as physical evidence and obtained as substances in the human body. Also included is a history of poisoning and toxicology.

☑ *Trace Evidence* by Max Houck. This book examines the common types of microscopic techniques used in forensic science, including scanning electron microscopy and analysis of microscopic evidence, such as dust, building materials, and other types of trace evidence.

☑ *Firearms and Fingerprints* by Edward Hueske, University of North Texas; supervising criminalist, Department of Public Safety of Arizona, 1983–96 (retired); Fellow, American Academy of Forensic Sciences; emeritus member of American Society of Crime Laboratory Directors (ASCLD). This book focuses on how firearms work, how impressions are created on bullets and casings, microscopic examination and comparison, and gunshot residue. The examination of other impression evidence, such as tire and shoe prints and fingerprints, is also included.

☑ *Crashes and Collapses* by Dr. Tom Bohan, J. D.; Diplomate, International Institute of Forensic Engineering Sciences; Founders Award recipient of the Engineering Sciences Section, American Academy of Forensic Sciences. This book covers forensic engineering and the investigation of accidents such as building and bridge collapses; accident reconstruction, and transportation disasters.

☑ *Fakes and Forgeries* by Dr. Suzanne Bell. This book provides an overview of questioned documents, identification of handwriting, counterfeiting, famous forgeries of art, and historical hoaxes.

Each volume begins with an overview of the subject, followed by a discussion of the history of the field and mention of the pioneers. Since the early forensic scientists were often active in several areas, the same names will appear in more than one volume. A section on the scientific principles and tools summarizes how forensic scientists working in that field acquire and apply their knowledge. With that foundation in place the forensic application of those principles is described to include important cases and the projected future in that area.

Finally, it is important to note that the volumes and the set as a whole are not meant to serve as a comprehensive textbook on the subject. Rather, the set is meant as a "pocket reference" best used for obtaining an overview of a particular subject while providing a list of resources for those needing or wanting more. The content is directed toward nonscientists, students, and members of the public who have been caught up in the current popularity of forensic science and want to move past fiction into forensic reality.

ACKNOWLEDGMENTS

I cannot remember a time when I was not writing; I guess the aphorism "writers write" is true. Although I do not think of myself as a "writer," apparently others do, and I thank them for taking the time to read my words. I also want to thank my wife for being patient with my mood swings while working on this project. I am grateful to Frank Darmstadt, my patient editor; Dorothy Cummings, project editor; Suzie Tibor, photo researcher; and the rest of the Facts On File team. Finally, I want to thank my agent, Jodie Rhodes, for keeping me in line; I am sorry I make you work so hard, Jodie.

INTRODUCTION

Shortly before midnight on June 12, 1994, two people lost their lives in a horrible crime, and as a result forensic science would never be the same. The murders of Ron Goldman and Nicole Brown Simpson captured the public's attention, much as other sensational killings had in the past. The wrongful conviction and eventual exoneration of Alfred Dreyfus for treason (1894) and Nicola Sacco and Bartolomeo Vanzetti's prosecution and execution for armed robbery and murder (1927 in Massachusetts), for example, were notable cases in their time. What ties these three—and other—cases together across more than 100 years? The scientific analysis of physical evidence was central in each case. In the Dreyfus case, known as the Dreyfus affair (or just *L'Affaire* in France at the time), the famed Alphonse Bertillon, inventor of the first forensic identification system, testified about questioned documents. Bertillon had no prior experience in the analysis of handwriting, and his reputation suffered when he overstepped his professional expertise. Author Émile Zola's famous open letter to the president of France, published in the newspaper *L'Aurore* with the title "J'Accuse. . . !" (French for "I Accuse. . . !"), brought the travesty of justice to light and helped to make it a public scandal.

Sacco and Vanzetti were tried and convicted of robbing and murdering two payroll clerks. The judgment was based on a variety of evidence but mostly on that concerning firearms. The evidence was equivocal, but the jury believed the prosecution's version, despite defense experts who claimed the bullets found in the slain clerks had not come from the alleged murder weapons. A cap that was alleged to be Sacco's was also offered as evidence. Foreshadowing the now-infamous glove in the Goldman-Simpson murders, the prosecution made Sacco try the cap on in court: It was too small. The prosecution nevertheless claimed it was Sacco's and continued to refer to it that way. Huge public outcries

The front page cover of the newspaper *L'Aurore,* Thursday, January 13, 1898, with the letter "J'Accuse. . .!", written by Émile Zola about the Dreyfus affair. The headline reads "I Accuse! Letter to the President of the Republic."

helped to bring some aspects of the case to light, demonstrating that political bias may have influenced the case (the defendants were anarchists). Sacco and Vanzetti's actual guilt remains a source of controversy.

Modern firearms tests on the alleged murder weapon, along with other historical evidence, point to their innocence.

More recently, the investigation, criminal trial, and controversial acquittal of O. J. Simpson for the murders of Ron Goldman and Nicole Simpson was also a highly publicized event, but with a difference. The main medium of information during the Dreyfus affair and the trials of Sacco and Vanzetti was the newspaper. Radio may have played a role in the Sacco and Vanzetti case, but the extent is unknown; the National Broadcasting Company began regular broadcasting in 1926, and the Columbia Broadcasting System began in 1927. The Goldman-Simpson murders, however, occured in an age of televised celebrity. The subsequent trial was also televised, offering a rare (at the time) view of a criminal prosecution. The drama, the horrific nature of the crime, and the fact that a celebrated athelete had been accused all led to a media frenzy, with the public paying rapt attention. The case centered on physical evidence, and the presentation of this evidence by some of the best-known forensic experts made for good theater; some experts were considered to be more celebrity than scientist. This intimate, broadly publicized look at crime scenes, forensic evidence, and the near-continual broadcasting of every aspect of the case brought forensic science into the limelight. New reality-based television shows sprung up and were quickly followed by fictionalized versions that became wildly popular (the *CSI* franchise, for example). Fantasy followed fact, and the public's perception of forensic science, sparked by reality, may have been skewed by the dramatic versions of criminal investigations and their ultimate solutions by science. Enrollment in forensic science educational programs soared, and new academic programs sprouted everywhere. Forensic science would never be the same.

Science versus Crime offers a reality check on the application of science to criminal investigations. You will find no scantily clad investigators, no dimly lit laboratories, no instant confessions between the covers of this book. What you will find, however, is far more fascinating: how forensic science really works to solve crimes. It is a wondrous profession for those with scientific ability and insatiable curiosity. I often joke to my students who express the concern of being "stuck in the lab all day" that you do get the same thing every day: variety. No two cases are the same, no two pieces of evidence are alike, and no two investigations follow the same path. My experience comes from having worked in the private sector for an instrumentation company as an applications specialist to forensic laboratories using our equipment, working in a county forensic laboratory and morgue as a trace evidence analyst and forensic anthropologist, being lucky enough to have worked at the Federal Bureau of Investigation Laboratory Division, and currently having the luxury of working in an outstanding academic environment at West Virginia University. I have been involved in some major cases, such as the Branch Davidian case in Waco, Texas, and the attack on the Pentagon on September 11, 2001. I have also worked on less-famous cases which were nevertheless important to those involved. All of these have taught me that forensic science deserves whatever glory it gets in the media, but we still have a lot to learn. This book, I hope, helps you understand what forensic science is and what can really be done to assist in the fight against crime.

After chapter 1, which orients you to the profession, chapter 2 covers some of the pioneers of forensic science; these are the (mostly) men who laid the groundwork for the science we use today. Chapter 3 provides a view of what evidence is and how it can be used in criminal investigations. All too often, the evidence is collected and analyzed without a consideration of what it is or what it can mean, ultimately. A bit of reflection can help us appreciate the potential of all forms of evidence. Chapters 4 ("Microscopy"), 5 ("Spectroscopy"), and 6 ("Chromatography") cover the main tools of the forensic laboratory—do not skip over them! A thorough knowledge of these methods means a more comprehensive use of the evidence in a case. Chapter 7 addresses the science of DNA, one of the most powerful tools in the forensic arsenal. Chapter 8, "Fingerprints," presents the first truly universal method of forensic identification. Much has been made lately of the reliability of fingerprints, as in the Madrid bombing case (2004); to know how any method can be improved, you must understand where it came from. Chapter 8, therefore, takes a bit more of a historical view. Chapter 9 covers the analysis of firearms, which are so prevalent in criminal cases. Finally, chapter 10 describes the communication of the scientist's findings, both in written form (reports) and oral (testimony). The best work in the world communicated poorly does no good. A companion book in this set, *Trace*

Evidence, covers the minute bits of evidence, such as hairs and fibers, that are routinely examined in cases of contact.

As Sherlock Holmes, the famous fictional detective, remarked in "A Scandal in Bohemia," "It is a capital mistake to theorize before one has data. Insensibly one begins to twist facts to suit theories, instead of theories to suit facts." *Science versus Crime* shows you how to collect those facts and then theorize from them.

Forensic Science:
In and Out of the Laboratory

*If you were a detective engaged in tracing a murder, would you expect
to find that the murderer had left his photograph behind at the place of
the crime, with his address attached? Or would you not necessarily have
to be satisfied with comparatively slight and obscure traces of the person
you were in search of?*

—Sigmund Freud

*One of the most admirable things about history is, that almost as a rule
we get as much information out of what it does not say as we get out of
what it does say. And so, one may truly and axiomatically aver this, to-
wit: that history consists of two equal parts; one of these halves is statements of fact, the other half is inference, drawn from the facts. . . . When
the practiced eye of the simple peasant sees the half of a frog projecting
above the water, he unerringly infers the half of the frog which he does
not see. To the expert student in our great science, history is a frog; half
of it is submerged, but he knows it is there, and he knows the shape of it.*

—Mark Twain,
"The Secret History of Eddypus, the World-Empire"

1

The *Oxford English Dictionary* lists one of the first uses of the phrase *forensic science* to describe "a mixed science." The early days of forensic science could certainly be called mixed, when science served justice by its application to questions before the court. Forensic science has grown as a profession and into a science in its own right. Given the public's interest in using science to solve crimes, it looks as if forensic science has an active future.

Forensic science describes the science of associating people, places, and things involved in criminal activities; these scientific disciplines assist in investigating and adjudicating criminal and civil cases. The discipline divides neatly into halves, like the term that describes it. Science is the collection of systematic methodologies used to increasingly understand the physical world. The word *forensic* is derived from the Latin *forum,* meaning "public." In ancient Rome, the Senate met in the forum, a public place where the political and policy issues of the day were discussed and debated; even today, high school or university teams that compete in debates or public speaking are called *forensics.* More technically, *forensic* means "as applied to public or legal concerns." Together, *forensic science* is an apt term for the profession of scientists whose work answers questions for the courts through reports and testimony.

FORENSIC SCIENCE LABORATORIES AND ORGANIZATIONS

It may seem odd, but there is no one structure for the organization of a forensic science laboratory. They vary by jurisdiction (the area for which they are responsible), agency, and history. The variation increases when laboratories in the United States are compared with those in other countries. The analyses and services that a forensic science laboratory provides also varies, based on the laboratory's budget, personnel, and equipment and the jurisdiction's crime rate.

Professional organizations cater to specific subgroups within forensic science, such as document examiners, medical examiners, fingerprint examiners, and so on. A table of professional organizations in forensic science with their Web addresses can be found in the "Further Reading" section.

FORENSIC SCIENCE LABORATORIES

The majority of forensic science laboratories in the United States are public, meaning they receive their money from and are operated by a federal, state, or local unit of government. Somewhere around 470 of these are in operation today. Some 30–50 private forensic science laboratories are also in operation.

Private Forensic Science Laboratories

Private forensic laboratories typically perform only one or two types of examinations, such as DNA analysis, drug analysis, or toxicology. Some "laboratories" are really a retired forensic scientist providing examinations in the specialties he or she performed while employed in a public forensic laboratory. A significant number of the (larger) private forensic laboratories are dedicated to DNA analysis; many of these also perform paternity testing (determining who the parents, usually the father, are). These private laboratories serve a needed function in the criminal justice system because they provide forensic services directly to persons involved or interested in crimes—that is, the suspects or defendants. Public forensic laboratories work only those cases submitted by police or other duly authorized law enforcement offices (Office of the State Attorney or Office of the Chief Medical Examiner, for example). They will not—and usually cannot—analyze evidence submitted by anyone else except as ordered by a judge or other appropriate official. Some public forensic laboratories will accept evidence from private citizens, however, and the fee or cost is subsidized by the jurisdiction (city, county, municipality) where the laboratory operates.

Public Forensic Science Laboratories

Public forensic science laboratories are financed and operated by a unit of government. Different jurisdictions have different models for where the laboratory appears in the governmental hierarchy. Federal laboratories have their own positions within the federal system.

Federal Government Forensic Science Laboratories

The federal forensic science laboratory that most people are familiar with is the Federal Bureau of Investigation (FBI) Laboratory. This is arguably the most famous forensic science laboratory in the world, but it is hardly the only federal forensic laboratory.

The FBI is a unit of the Department of Justice. It has one operational laboratory and a research center (Forensic Science Research and Training Center) near their Training Academy in Quantico, Virginia. The FBI Laboratory assists the investigations of its own Special Agents. The FBI Laboratory will, upon request, analyze evidence that has not already been examined by any duly authorized law enforcement agency or forensic science laboratory.

The History of the FBI Laboratory

In the 1920s, a young, newly appointed Bureau of Investigation director named J. Edgar Hoover recognized the importance of scientific analysis in criminal matters. He encouraged the bureau to remain abreast of scientific advancements and use them where appropriate. In 1930, the bureau established a criminology library and began collecting and publishing uniformed crime statistics, a task previously assigned to the International Association of Chiefs of Police. Bureau agents-in-training attended lectures on such subjects as fingerprint comparison, handwriting comparison, and ballistics.

At the time, however, the bureau did not have its own laboratory or scientific staff. Outside experts were hired on a case-by-case basis. This approach was neither efficient nor cost-effective. The infamous St. Valentine's Day Massacre on February 14, 1929, led to the establishment of the Scientific Crime Detection Laboratory at Northwestern University in Chicago. Hoover encouraged bureau special agents in charge to subscribe to the laboratory's *American Journal of Police Science,* and he contributed articles to the journal. Bureau agents also attended training at the Chicago crime laboratory. Special Agent Charles Appel, a staunch supporter of Hoover's vision of fighting crime with science, attended training classes in a number of disciplines, including serology, toxicology, handwriting and typewriting analysis, and moulage (the making

The Drug Enforcement Administration (DEA) is responsible for investigating major criminal drug operations; it also helps stop drugs from other countries entering the United States. The DEA has a network of seven drug laboratories throughout the United States: Washington, D.C.; Miami, Florida; Chicago, Illinois; Dallas, Texas; San Francisco, California; New York, New York; and San Diego, California. They also maintain the Special Testing and Research Laboratory, in Chantilly, Virginia. The DEA laboratories support investigations with local or regional law enforcement and in joint operations.

of impressions or casts for casework and courtroom testimony). While applying his new knowledge to bureau casework, Appel continued to seek out additional training and educational opportunities. At the same time, he researched the development of a crime laboratory.

On July 7, 1932, in a memorandum to Hoover, Appel proposed a separate division within the Bureau to handle so-called crime prevention work and to oversee a "criminological research laboratory." In another memo two weeks later, Appel outlined his vision for the laboratory. He envisioned that the Bureau of Investigation would play a central role in American law enforcement by serving as a source of information and criminological support. Hoover shared and supported this vision, which has served as a cornerstone for the FBI's work throughout its history.

In September 1932, the birth of this vision was realized when an ultraviolet light machine, a microscope, a moulage kit, a wiretapping kit, photographic supplies, chemicals, a drawing board, and other office equipment and supplies were moved into room 802 of the Old Southern Railway Building at 13th Street and Pennsylvania Avenue, N.W., Washington, D.C. Initially named the Criminology Laboratory, its official birth date was established as November 24, 1932. In its first year of operation, the FBI Laboratory performed approximately 963 examinations.

The Bureau of Alcohol, Tobacco, Firearms, and Explosives (ATF) has three regional laboratories located in Ammendale, Maryland (outside Washington, D.C.); Atlanta, Georgia; and Walnut Creek, California (near San Francisco). The new Fire Research Laboratory, the largest of its kind in the world, was built in conjunction with the Ammendale laboratory. The name of the agency would seem to indicate what it analyzes—alcohol, tobacco, and firearms—but the ATF laboratories also are renowned for their expertise in fire-scene analysis and explosives. ATF has enhanced its analytical offerings and now offers a nearly full range of forensic services.

The United States Secret Service Laboratory (USSSL) in Washington, D.C., has two main functions. First is counterfeiting and fraud, including counterfeit currency, fraudulent credit cards, and related documents. The USSSL has one of the world's largest libraries of ink standards, and questioned document analysis is one of their primary functions. The other function is in support of the Secret Service's role in executive protection. The laboratory researches and develops countermeasures and technologies for the protection of the president and other officials. The U.S. Secret Service is a part of the U.S. Department of Homeland Security.

Another agency that may not be associated normally with a forensic laboratory is the Internal Revenue Service (IRS), which has a laboratory in Chicago, Illinois. The IRS Laboratory specializes in questioned document analysis, especially inks and papers. Authentication of signatures on tax returns, fraudulent documentation relating to taxation, and other forms of fraud with the aim of avoiding federal taxes are their bread and butter.

The U.S. Fish and Wildlife Service (USFWS) operates a unique forensic science laboratory in Ashland, Oregon. The USFWS Laboratory performs animal-oriented forensic analyses, and its mission is to support the efforts of the USFWS's investigators who patrol the national parks. The laboratory supports the FWS agents in their investigations of poachers and people who kill or injure endangered species. The laboratory examines evidence involving animals and has specialized expertise in the identification of hooves, hairs, feathers, bone, and other animal tissues. The laboratory works with similar investigative agencies from other countries to track poachers and people who traffic in animal parts, such as bear gallbladders (in Asia, bear gall is thought to improve sexual potency) and elephant ivory. The laboratory is a sophisticated facility that has some of the world's leading experts in animal forensic science.

While the United States Postal Service (USPS) is not strictly a federal agency, it is considered to be a quasi-federal agency. The USPS has a laboratory in the Washington, D.C., area that supports the service's efforts to combat postal fraud. It does this through the analysis of questioned document, fingerprints, and trace evidence (for example, hairs, fibers, and particles).

State and Local Forensic Science Laboratories

Every state in the United States has at least one forensic science laboratory. State forensic science laboratories traditionally are housed in one of two places: law enforcement or health departments. Law enforcement is the most prevalent. The bulk of nonfederal public forensic laboratories are part of a state or local law enforcement agency. The remainder are located in health departments or some other scientific agency within the governmental hierarchy. In all states there is a statewide laboratory or laboratory system that is operated by the state police or the state department of justice. Some states' laboratories are independent of the state law enforcement system, such as in Virginia. In California, the state department of justice operates an extensive network of state financed laboratories, whereas West Virginia has a single laboratory that serves the whole state.

Most states also have laboratories operated by a local governmental unit, like a large city or county. For example, in Maryland some counties have laboratories under the jurisdiction of the county police department, separate from the state system. In California, Los Angeles has a county laboratory that has some overlapping jurisdiction with the city laboratory. In Michigan, the Detroit City Police Department has its own forensic science laboratory, but the rest of Wayne County surrounding Detroit is serviced by the state police laboratories. This confusing hodge-podge of politics and geography may seem wasteful, but it has developed because of real societal needs, such as population levels, crime rates, and economics.

FORENSIC SCIENCE LABORATORY SERVICES

Not all forensic science laboratories offer the same types of analyses. In a state laboratory system, for example, typically one laboratory will offer a full range of forensic science services and the regional laboratories provide limited services (for example, fingerprints, firearms, and drug analysis). It is important to note that "full service" does not always mean "every service"—a laboratory may not analyze gunshot residue analysis, yet it may still describe itself as "full service."

Evidence Control and Intake

Receiving, managing, and returning evidence is a central function of any forensic science laboratory. In a small laboratory, one employee may be assigned to fulfill this function, while in a larger one, several people may work in an evidence unit. The evidence must be stored in a secured area to ensure its integrity; depending on the amount of casework, this area may be a room or an entire building. Evidence is submitted by a police officer or investigator who fills out paperwork describing the evidence and the type of examinations requested. The laboratory will assign a unique laboratory number to the case; in modern laboratories, this is done through a computerized laboratory information management system (LIMS). Each item of evidence is labeled with the unique laboratory number, along with other identifying information, such as the item number. The documentation of the location of evidence takes place from the time it is collected at the crime scene until it is presented in court; this documentation is called the chain of custody. When evidence is transferred from one scientist to another, the first scientist lists the items to be transferred, prints his or her name, writes the date and time of the transfer, and signs the form. The person receiving the evidence prints his or her name and also signs the form. The chain of custody form permanently accompanies the laboratory case file. Much as a business must have a system of inventory control to know what goods it has and how much it has sold, so too must a forensic science laboratory have a system for inventorying evidence.

LIMS uses computerized systems that help laboratories keep track of evidence and information about analyses. Think of them as databases that generate labels, barcodes, or other tags to identify and inventory evidence. This automation greatly assists large laboratories where perhaps tens of thousands of evidence items flow through the facility each year—the FBI Laboratory, for example, performs more than 2 million examinations per year.

Analytical Sections

Evidence from a case is assigned to one or more forensic units within the laboratory for analysis. Each unit then assigns an individual scientist to be responsible for the evidence and its analysis. Several scientists may be assigned to the same case, each responsible for their own specific analyses (DNA, fingerprints, firearms, and so forth). Conversely, one item of evidence may be analyzed by several scientists in turn. Take the example of a threatening letter, one that allegedly contains anthrax or some other contagious material. The envelope and the letter could be subjected to the following examinations, in order:

- disease diagnosis, to determine if evidence really contains the suspected contagion

- trace evidence, for hairs or fibers in the envelope or stuck to the adhesives (stamp, closure, tape used to seal it)

- DNA, from saliva on the stamp or the envelope closure

- questioned documents, for the paper, lettering, and other aspects of the form of the letter

- ink analysis, to determine what was used to write the message, address, etc.

- handwriting, typewriter, or printer analysis, as appropriate

- latent fingerprints

- content analysis, to evaluate the nature of the writer's intent and other investigative clues

The order of the exams is important: The first scientist does not want to destroy the evidence the next scientist needs to analyze. As an example, a full-service laboratory analytical section might contain the following sections:

- photography

- biology/DNA

- firearms and toolmarks

- footwear and tire treads

- questioned documents

- friction ridge analysis

- chemistry/illegal drugs

- toxicology

- trace evidence

The term *trace evidence* is specific to forensic science; it may also be called *criminalistics, microchemistry,* or *microanalysis.* This area generally encompasses the analysis of hairs, fibers, soils, glass, paints, plastics, ignitable liquids, explosives, building materials, inks, and dyes. The common link between all these evidence materials is that they often appear as small pieces of the original source; therefore a microscope is used to examine and analyze them. The microscope may be integrated into another scientific instrument so that the very small samples can be analyzed.

The term *criminalistics* is sometimes used to describe certain areas of forensic science. *Criminalistics* is a word imported into English from the German *kriminalistik.* The word was coined to capture the various aspects of applying scientific and technological methods to the investigation and resolution of legal matters. In California and western states in the United States, forensic scientists working in forensic science laboratories may refer to themselves as "criminalists." Criminalistics is generally thought of as the branch of forensic science that involves collection and analysis of physical evidence generated by criminal activity. It includes areas such as drugs, firearms and toolmarks, fingerprints, blood and body fluids, footwear, and trace evidence. *Trace evidence* is a term of art that means different things to different people. It might include fire and explosive residues, glass, soils, hairs, fibers, paints, plastics and other polymers, wood, metals, and chemicals.

Sometimes forensic laboratories offer services other than those listed above, such as bloodstain pattern analysis, entomology, anthropology, or other specialties. Smaller laboratories that have only an occasional need for these services may submit the evidence to the FBI laboratory, a private laboratory, or a local specialist.

SPECIALIZED AREAS OF FORENSIC SCIENCE

The services provided by a local or state forensic laboratory are determined by the needs of the people it serves; not all laboratories provide all services. Some forensic sciences are so specialized that only a relatively few practice them. This section provides short overviews of some of the forensic specialties that may—or may not—occur in a forensic laboratory but are nevertheless important to investigations and solving crimes.

Forensic Pathology

Back in the 1970s and 1980s, when the *Quincy, M.E.* television show was popular, many people considered forensic pathology and forensic science as the same thing—a misconception that persists to this day. The forensic pathologist is a medical doctor, specially trained in clinical and anatomical pathology (pathology is the study of diseases and trauma), whose function is to determine the cause and manner of death in cases where the death occurred under suspicious or unknown circumstances. This often involves a teamwork approach with the autopsy or postmortem examination of the body as the central function. Forensic pathologists or their investigators are often called to death scenes to make some preliminary observations, including an estimate of the time since death.

Forensic Anthropology

Forensic anthropology is a branch of physical anthropology encompassing the study of humans, their biology, and their ancestors. Forensic anthropology deals with identifying people who cannot be identified through fingerprints, photographs, or other similar means. Typically, forensic anthropologists analyze skeletal remains to determine if they are human and, if so, the age, sex, height, and other characteristics of the deceased.

Forensic anthropologists are central to the reconstruction and identification of victims in mass fatalities, such as bombings and airplane crashes. Working closely with pathologists, dentists, and others, forensic anthropologists aid in the identification of victims who otherwise might not be found.

Forensic Dentistry

Sometimes called forensic odontology, forensic dentistry serves a number of purposes to the forensic sciences. These include identification of human remains in mass disasters (the enamel in teeth is the hardest material produced by the body, and intact teeth are often found at disaster sites), postmortem X-rays of the teeth can be compared to antemortem X-rays, and the comparison of bite marks.

Forensic Engineering

Forensic engineers analyze why things fail—everything from faulty toasters that electrocute people to buildings and bridges that crumble apart and kill many people. For example, forensic engineering assisted greatly in the analysis of the September 11 attacks on the World Trade Center and the Pentagon. Forensic engineers may also help to reconstruct traffic accidents. Based on tire skid marks, damage to vehicles and surrounding items, and the laws of physics, they can determine path, direction, speed, and the type of collision that occurred.

Toxicology

Toxicologists analyze body fluids and tissues to determine if toxic substances, such as drugs or poisons, are present. If they identify such a substance, they then determine how much is present and what effect, if any, the substance might have had to impair, hurt, or kill the person. Forensic toxicologists work closely with forensic pathologists. Many of the cases forensic toxicologists work on involve drunk driving or operating under the influence, cases in which the blood or breath alcohol content must be determined.

Behavioral Sciences

Popularized by television series such as *Profiler* and films such as the award-winning *Silence of the Lambs,* forensic psychiatrists and psychologists do not only hunt serial killers. They also study developmental and mental causes of an individual's criminal activity, counsel victims, and determine a person's competency to stand trial and aid in one's own defense. Competency to stand trial is a recurring issue because insanity has been a common legal defense. To complicate things, each state has its own standards for what constitutes insanity. The central question is whether or not the defendant was in a mental capacity to know right actions from wrong ones at the time of the crime.

Behavioral forensic scientists also assist investigations of serial crimes by creating psychological profiles of the criminals. People tend to act in predictable patterns when they commit crimes, and the discovery of these behavioral patterns can provide clues to the personality of the offender. Behavioral scientists may also be called upon to help in interviewing or interrogating suspects in crimes. Although profiling can provide useful information about whom the police should look for, it is not an exact science by any means.

Questioned Documents

A questioned document is just that—a document whose authenticity is in question. The examination of questioned documents (QD) is a complicated and wide-ranging area of study often requiring a great deal of examination, mentoring, and training. To determine the source or authenticity of a particular document, QD examiners may be required to analyze any or all of the following: handwriting, typewriting, printed documents, inks, and paper. Documents also may be examined to detect erasures, obliterations, forgeries, alterations, and counterfeiting (mostly currency).

Accreditation, Standardization, and Certification

Accreditation is the process by which a laboratory guarantees that its services are offered with a certain degree of quality, integrity, and assurance. The accreditation process is extensive, rigorous, and demanding for the laboratory that undertakes it. The laboratory and its staff first undergo a comprehensive self-study entailing a long checklist of requirements. The laboratory then applies for accreditation. The accrediting agency (see below) sends out a trained team to perform an on-site evaluation. If the laboratory passes evaluation, it becomes accredited. It is important to remember that accreditation says nothing about the competence of the individual forensic scientists who work at the laboratory; that is certification, discussed later. Being accredited does mean that the laboratory meets certain minimum criteria for the facilities, security, training, equipment, quality assurance and control, and other essentials.

In the United States, forensic science laboratories can be accredited through two agencies. The first is the American Society of Crime Laboratory Directors (ASCLD) Laboratory Accreditation Board (ASCLD-LAB). The ASCLD is a professional organization of forensic science laboratory directors; ASCLD-LAB is a separate but related organization. Reaccreditation is required every five years in order to maintain the laboratory's status. The other agency by which forensic laboratories can seek accreditation is the International Standards Organization (ISO).

Standards play a major role in helping laboratories become accredited. A standard can take two forms. First, it can be a written standard, which is like a very specific recipe and has to be followed exactly to get the proper result. The American Society for Testing and Materials, International (ASTM) publishes standards for a wide variety of sciences, including forensic science. These standards are written by groups of experts in the field who come to agreement on the acceptable way to perform a certain analysis. Second, a standard can be a physical thing, such as a one-gram cube of pure copper. Physical standards like this are called reference materials because scientists refer to them when analyzing other samples—for example, if a specimen is 99.999 percent pure copper, then its properties are known, as is how it ought to react in an experiment. If the reference material has been tested extensively by many methods, it can be issued as a certified reference material (CRM). CRMs come with certificates guaranteeing their purity or quality. The National Institute of Standards and Technology (NIST) is the U.S. government agency that issues CRMs.

EDUCATION AND TRAINING OF FORENSIC SCIENTISTS

Science is the heart of forensic science. Court decisions such as *Daubert v. Merrill Dow* (1993) have reinforced this issue. A forensic scientist must be well-versed in the methods and requirements of good science in general and in the specific techniques used in the particular disciplines being practiced. Additionally, the forensic scientist must be familiar with the rules of evidence and court procedures in the relevant jurisdictions. The knowledge, skills, and aptitudes needed in these areas are gained by a combination of formal education, formal training, and experience.

Education

In the past, forensic scientists were recruited from the ranks of chemistry or biology majors in college. Little or no education was provided in the forensic sciences themselves—all of that was learned on the job. Since the middle of the 20th century, however, undergraduate and then graduate programs in forensic science have been offered by a handful of colleges and universities in the United States. The early bachelor's degree programs provided a strong chemical, mathematical, biological science, and physical science background coupled with applied laboratory experience in the analysis of evidence, with classes in law and criminal procedure mixed in. These programs also offered opportunities for a practicum in a functioning forensic science laboratory to see how science was applied in forensic laboratories. The American Academy of Forensic Sciences (AAFS) Web site (www.aafs.org) lists more than 40 programs that offer a bachelor's degree with some level of forensic emphasis.

In the past 20 years or so, graduate degrees, particularly at the master's level, have become the norm. About two dozen graduate (M.A., M.S., or Ph.D.) programs in the United States are listed on the AAFS Web site. These typically require a bachelor's degree in a science and then teach the applications of the science to forensic work, as well as classes in relevant aspects of law, criminal investigation, and criminal justice. A research component is also generally required.

"Forensic Sciences: Review of Status and Needs," a published report from the National Institute of Justice in 1999, noted the following:

> [The educational and training needs] of the forensic community are immense. Training of newcomers to the field, as well as providing continuing education for seasoned professionals, is vital to ensuring that crime laboratories deliver the best possible service to the criminal justice system. Forensic scientists must stay up-to-date as new technology, equipment, methods, and techniques are developed. While training

programs exist in a variety of forms, there is need to broaden their scope and build on existing resources.

The review made a number of recommendations, including seeking mechanisms for

- accreditation/certification of forensic academic training programs/institutions,

- setting national consensus standards of education in the forensic sciences, and

- ensuring that all forensic scientists have professional orientations to the field, formal quality-assurance training, and expert-witness training.

The Technical Working Group on Education and Training in Forensic Science (TWGED) was created in response to the needs expressed by the justice system, including the forensic science and law enforcement communities, to establish models for training and education in forensic science. West Virginia University, in conjunction with the National Institute of Justice, sponsored the TWGED, which was made up of more than 50 forensic scientists, educators, laboratory directors, and professionals. The TWGED drafted a guide addressing qualifications for a career in forensic science, an undergraduate curriculum in forensic science, graduate education in forensic science, training and continuing education, and forensic science careers outside of the traditional forensic science laboratory.

Seeing this as an opportunity, the AAFS initiated the Forensic Science Education Program Accreditation Commission (FEPAC) as a standing committee of the Academy. The FEPAC drafted accreditation standards for forensic education programs based on the TWGED guidelines. FEPAC's mission is to maintain and enhance the quality of forensic science education through a formal evaluation and recognition of college-level academic programs. The commission's primary function is to develop and maintain standards and to administer an accreditation program that recognizes and distinguishes high-quality undergraduate and graduate forensic science programs.

A pilot program of six forensic educational institutions was run in 2003, with open applications for accreditation accepted in 2004. By 2007, 16 programs at 14 institutions had been accredited by FEPAC. For more information about TWGED and FEPAC, visit www.aafs.org.

Formal Training

Educational programs are not, however, designed to provide training so that a graduate can start working cases on his or her first day in a forensic science laboratory. Formal training begins once a scientist is employed by a forensic science laboratory. New scientists are normally hired as specialists; they will learn how to analyze evidence in one or a group of related areas. Thus, someone may be hired as a drug analyst, a trace-evidence analyst, or a firearms examiner. Training requires a period of apprenticeship during which the newly hired scientist works closely with an experienced scientist. The length of time for training varies widely with the discipline and the laboratory. For example, a drug chemist may train for three to six months before taking cases, while a DNA analyst may train for one to two years, and a questioned document examiner may spend up to three years in apprenticeship. Training usually involves mock casework as well as assisting in real cases. Ideally it also includes proficiency testing at intervals and mock trials at the end of the training.

On the Job Training: Experience

Some people say that no one really learns to drive a car until after one gets a license, when the experience of the everyday driving situations improves a driver's skills—or worsens them. The same could be said for forensic science. After education and training, casework begins, and only then do forensic scientists learn how to be effective. Time and resource-management skills develop, and the pressure of testifying in court hones one's abilities. Learning how to "hurry up and wait" to testify, how to handle the media (or not), and about dealing with harried attorneys are all part of a forensic scientist's growth. These are aspects of the career that are difficult to convey to someone who has not experienced them.

ISSUES OF EVIDENCE

This is why someone wants to become a forensic scientist: to analyze evidence. The science and method of this process fills the rest of this book.

But besides the routine analysis of evidence, there are many important aspects other than science that affect how evidence is analyzed:

- *Chain of custody.* The forensic scientist must be constantly aware of the requirements of the chain of custody. Evidence can be rendered inadmissible if the chain of custody is not properly constructed and maintained.

- *Turn-around time.* There are federal and state "speedy trial" laws requiring that an accused person is brought to trial within a specified window of time after arrest; this is usually 180 days but may vary with the jurisdiction. If the forensic science laboratory cannot analyze and report on evidence in a timely manner, the accused may be released for failure of the government to provide a speedy trial.

- *Preservation and spoilage.* Forensic scientists have a duty to preserve as much of the evidence as is practical in a given case and to ensure that the evidence is not spoiled or ruined. In some cases, so little evidence exists that there is only one chance for analysis. In such cases, the prosecutor and defense attorney should be informed before the analysis takes place.

- *Sampling.* There are many cases where there is so much evidence that sampling becomes an issue. This often happens with large drug cases where there may be hundreds or thousands of similar exhibits; it can also be true of bloodstains, fibers, or any type of evidence. The opposite may also be true: These may be insufficient samples for complete or repeat analysis. Finally, there may be cases where any type of analysis is destructive and there is no opportunity for reanalysis.

- *Reports.* Every laboratory has protocols for writing laboratory reports, but a surprising lack of uniformity exists from laboratory to laboratory. Some laboratories mandate complete reports for each case, whereas others have bare-bones reports with a minimum of description and explanation. Reports of forensic science analysis are scientific reports and should be complete like any other scientific report.

EXPERT TESTIMONY

Being a competent analytical scientist is only half the battle in a forensic science laboratory. The forensic scientist must also be able to explain his or her findings to a judge or jury in a court of law. This is one of the key factors that distinguish the forensic sciences.

There are a number of definitions of an expert. For forensic science purposes, an expert may thought of as a person who possesses a combination of knowledge, skills, and aptitudes in a particular area that permit him or her to draw inferences from facts that the average person would not be competent to do. In short, an expert knows more about something than the average person and has the credentials to prove it. An expert does not have to possess a Ph.D. Many experts have accumulated expertise over years of experience and may not have much education. For example, suppose that a person is killed while driving his car because the brakes failed and he crashed into a tree. If an average group of people were to inspect the brakes of the car, they would not be competent to determine why the brakes failed or even if they did. This would require the services of an expert mechanic to examine the brake system and then make conclusions about if, why, and how the brakes failed. A difference exists, however, between an expert and a forensic scientist: A mechanic is not a forensic scientist.

2

History and Pioneers

Early examples of what we would now call forensic science are scattered throughout history. In *The Washing Away of Wrongs,* a text about 13th-century forensic medicine in China, the first recorded forensic entomology case is discussed. A man was stabbed near a rice field, and the investigating magistrate came to the scene the following day. He told the field hands to lay down their sickles, used to cut the rice stalks, on the floor in front of them. Blow flies, which are attracted to rotting flesh, were drawn to tiny traces of blood on one of the sickles—and none of the others. The owner of that sickle was confronted and ultimately confessed.

Forensic science officially emerged during the 19th century at a time when many factors were influencing society. European and American cities were growing in size and complexity. People accustomed to knowing everyone in their neighborhood or village were increasingly encountering new and different people. Transients and crooks, as well as decent people, traveled from city to city, committing crimes and becoming invisible in the crowds. Repeat criminal offenders who wanted to escape the law only had to move to a new town and give a false name, and no one might be the wiser. It became important for the government to be able to identify citizens because they might not be trusted to provide their true identities.

Whether fictional or real, the following pioneers in forensic science helped to shape the profession. Some, who were fictional, framed the profession through concepts that are now familiar to the forensic science community, such as the fact that the most minute amount of evidence can change the course of an investigation. Others, who were real, were practitioners who improved the science through new methods and applications. Either way, the field of forensic science is built on the works—both real and fictional—of these visionaries.

In this shifting society, the fictional detective story was born. Acting as loners, working with but outside the established police force, these literary characters helped to define what would become forensic science. One of the first of these "fictional pioneers" was a 32-year-old assistant editor in Richmond, Virginia.

EDGAR ALLAN POE (1809–1849): A PIONEER OF DETECTIVE FICTION

Born in Boston and educated in Virginia and England, Edgar Allan Poe became the father of the modern American mystery story. As a young man, he worked for several publications as both editor and writer, his success as the former coinciding with his growth as the latter. His early work was highly praised but did not create enough income for him and his wife (his young cousin) to live on. His reputation did help sales, however, as did macabre tales of suspense such as "The Fall of the House of Usher." Poe published other trademark tales of horror, including "The Tell-Tale Heart" and "The Pit and the Pendulum." His haunting poem "The Raven," published in 1845, assured his literary fame.

Mystery and crime stories as they appear today did not emerge until Poe introduced mystery fiction's first fictional detective, Auguste C. Dupin, in the 1841 story "The Murders in the Rue Morgue." Poe continued his exploits in stories such as "The Mystery of Marie Roget" (1842) and "The Purloined Letter" (1845). Dupin is a man of singular intelligence and logical process. His powers of observation are acute and seemingly superhuman. In "The Murders in the Rue Morgue," during a

A 1904 photo of an 1848 daguerreotype of American author Edgar Allan Poe. He is routinely credited with creating the genre of the detective novel. *(Courtesy of the Library of Congress)*

quiet walk with his unnamed friend in the story, Dupin suddenly says, "He is a very little fellow, that's true, and would do better for the Theatre des Varietes." His companion calmly agrees—and then is shocked that Dupin has apparently read his mind! He demands to know how Dupin knew that he was thinking of Chantilly, an actor of short stature. Dupin claims it was a fruit seller, who had bumped into his companion just a few minutes prior:

"We had been talking of horses, if I remember aright. . . . As we crossed into this street, a fruiterer, with a large basket upon his head, brushing quickly past us, thrust you upon a pile of paving-stones collected at a spot where the causeway is undergoing repair. You stepped upon one of the loose fragments, slipped . . . appeared vexed or sulky, muttered a few words, turned to look at the pile, and then proceeded in silence. . . ."

"You kept your eyes upon the ground—glancing, with a petulant expression, at the holes and ruts in the pavement (so that I saw you were still thinking of the stones), until we reached the little alley called Lamartine, which has been paved. . . . Here your countenance brightened up, and, perceiving your lips move, I could not doubt that you murmured the word "stereotomy," a term very affectedly applied to this species of pavement. I knew that you could not say to yourself 'stereotomy' without being brought to think of atomies, and thus of the theories of Epicurus; and since, when we discussed this subject not very long ago, I mentioned to you how singularly, yet with how little notice, the vague guesses of that noble Greek had met with confirmation in the late nebular cosmogony, I felt that you could not avoid casting your eyes upward to the great nebula in Orion, and I certainly expected that you would do so. You did look up; and I was now assured that I correctly followed your steps. . . . It was clear, therefore, that you would not fail to combine the two ideas of Orion and Chantilly. That you did combine them I saw by the character of the smile which passed over your lips. . . . I saw you draw yourself up to your full height. I was then sure that you reflected upon the diminutive figure of Chantilly."

Dupin's conclusions are not pure logic; there is a good amount of intuition and "educated guessing" to his mental gymnastics. A hallmark of later fictional—and real—detectives, creativity is central to good sleuthing.

The two men read of the horrible murder of a woman and her daughter in their apartment on the Rue Morgue. The bodies have been mutilated and the apartment torn to shreds. Neighbors talk of a foreigner speaking in a guttural language no one understands. Dupin comments on the sensationalism of the newspaper story and the ineptness of the police to his companion:

"They have fallen into the gross but common error of confounding the unusual with the abstruse. But it is by these deviations from the plane of the ordinary, that reason feels its way, if at all, in its search for the true. In investigations such as we are now pursuing, it should not be so

The Needle-in-a-Haystack Method

The terrible fate of the Chardon family was discovered a week and a half before Christmas in 1834. A widow and her son were found brutally murdered in their Paris home: She had been stabbed to death, and his head had been cut open by a hatchet. Initial suspicion fell on the son's acquaintances, but the case turned cold. On New Year's Eve, the attempted murder of a bank courier was reported. The courier had been sent to collect funds from a man named Mahossier. The courier had found the address, knocked, and entered. The young man was grabbed from behind and stabbed in the back, but he managed to wrestle free from his attacker and cry for help. His attacker fled.

The Sûreté, Paris's counterpart to London's Scotland Yard, assigned the same detective, named Canler, to both cases. Canler proceeded to do what detectives did in those days: He began a search of every low-rent hotel and rooming house in Paris for a guest register with the name Mahossier. He found a hotel that had registered a Mahossier, but the proprietors could not provide a description. Inquiring about the guest just below Mahossier—named François—Canler heard a description that reminded him of a criminal who had just been jailed. Canler interrogated François and found that he knew Mahossier and had helped him with the attempt on the bank courier's life. However, he did not know his real name. Back to the streets went Canler. He visited the usual criminal hangouts and shopped the description of Mahossier, only to discover his real name was Gaillard. Canler found poetry and letters in another hotel room and compared it with the handwriting from Mahossier; they were the same.

Meanwhile, François had been to trial and was convicted. Canler decided to visit François on his way to prison. Desperate to make good much asked 'what has occurred?' as 'what has occurred that has never occurred before?' In fact, the facility with which I shall arrive, or have arrived, at the solution of this mystery, is in the direct ratio of its apparent insolubility in the eyes of the police."

somehow, François told Canler he could help him with the Chardon killings. He had been drinking with a man who claimed to be the Chardons' killer while another man kept watch. The killer said his name was Gaillard.

Gaillard's accomplice in the Chardon case was another prisoner who confessed once he was confronted with Gaillard's murderous nature. The man told Canler of Gaillard's aunt and where she lived. Canler visited the aunt who told police she feared for her life from her nephew. His real name? Pierre-François Lacenaire. As will be seen later, this is why it was so difficult for police to track criminals in the days before our modern electronic communications. A warrant went out for Lacenaire's arrest.

At the beginning of February, Canler received notice that Lacenaire had been arrested for passing forged money in another town. A canny understanding of the criminal psyche led Canler to suggest to Lacenaire that his accomplices had implicated him in his crimes. Lacenaire refused to believe his accomplices would "squeal" on him; in prison, however, he asked around about whether that was true. Friends of François took poorly to the impugning of their fellow criminal and beat Lacenaire mercilessly. When he was released from the prison hospital, he confessed his crimes to Canler and implicated both his accomplices. Lacenaire was executed a year later, in January 1835.

This case demonstrates the criminal investigative methodology in place in the early 1800s—dogged, persistent searching. Little or no physical evidence was used because the police disregarded it as "circumstantial"—that is, abstract and irrelevant. The pioneering successes discussed later in this book changed all that and increasingly brought science into investigations and the courtroom.

The amateur detectives secure the permission of the prefect of police (like the chief of a modern-day police force) to assist in the investigation. Although they assist the police, Dupin is critical of their methods:

> "The Parisian police, so much extolled for acumen, are cunning, but no more. There is no method in their proceedings, beyond the method of the moment. They make a vast parade of measures; but, not infrequently, these are . . . ill-adapted to the objects proposed. . . . The results attained by them are not unfrequently surprising, but for the most part, are brought about by simple diligence and activity. . . . Thus there is such a thing as being too profound."

Poe's detective goes on to solve "The Murders in the Rue Morgue" in a style that sets the stage for fictional detectives for decades to come. Real detectives of the time did employ "simple diligence and activity" in their investigations. They had little knowledge of forensic evidence as detectives do today and slogged along doggedly in pursuit of the slightest clue. The true case of the French criminal Pierre-François Lacenaire demonstrates the "needle-in-a-haystack" method used to catch criminals at the time.

In February 1847, Poe's wife, Virginia, died of consumption (usually meaning tuberculosis). Poe was devastated by her death, and his life spiraled into bouts of alcohol abuse and depression. In October 1849, Edgar Allan Poe died in Baltimore, age 40, of curious causes most often attributed to his alcoholism.

SIR ARTHUR CONAN DOYLE (1859–1930): THE CREATOR OF SHERLOCK HOLMES

Born in Edinburgh, Scotland, Arthur Conan Doyle studied to be a doctor at the University of Edinburgh. While at medical school, Doyle had been greatly inspired by one of his professors, John Bell, who displayed an uncanny deductive reasoning in diagnosing diseases. After he graduated, Doyle set up a small medical practice at Southsea in Hampshire. He was not entirely successful as a medical doctor, but his lack of patients gave him time to write. Doyle had been so influenced by Bell that he incorporated his former professor's ideas and patterns of thinking in his most famous character. Sherlock Holmes was introduced in *A Study in*

Scarlet (1887), and reappeared in *The Sign of Four* in 1890. It was not until *Strand* magazine published a series of stories, later published as *The Adventures of Sherlock Holmes*, that Holmes became an instant hit, and the public clamored for more stories of the consulting detective and Dr. John H. Watson, his friend and confidant.

From 1891 to 1893, *Strand* published stories featuring Holmes and Watson, all avidly followed by the public. Doyle, however, became weary of writing the detective stories and decided to end his character's career. In "The Final Problem" (1893), Holmes and his longtime archenemy, Professor James Moriarty, killed each other in a battle at Reichenbach Falls. The public rebelled, and Doyle was forced to bring Holmes back from the dead. Holmes and Watson continued their adventures in *The Hound of the Baskervilles* (1902). More books and stories were published until *The Case-Book of Sherlock Holmes* in 1927. In all, Holmes and Watson were featured in four novels and 56 stories during Doyle's lifetime.

Like Dupin, Holmes possessed superior intelligence, keen observation skills, and dogged persistence. These are the hallmarks of fictional detectives. Real forensic investigators use intuition and deduction as well.

LAMBERT-ADOLPHE-JACQUES QUÉTELET (1796–1874): THE FATHER OF MODERN STATISTICS

A gifted Belgian mathematician, astronomer, and statistician, Adolphe Quételet applied statistical reasoning to social phenomena, something that had not been done before. His work profoundly influenced the European social sciences. The history of the social sciences from the late 1830s onwards is, in large measure, the story of the application and refinement of ideas about the operation of probability in human affairs. These ideas about probability gained widespread currency in intellectual and government circles through Quételet's writings. His lifelong interest in gathering and interpreting statistics began in earnest in the early 1820s, when he was employed by the government of the Low Countries (modern Belgium, Luxembourg, and the Netherlands) to improve the collection and interpretation of census data. European governments had made practical use of probability well before the 1820s; however,

Quételet was convinced that probability influenced the course of human affairs more profoundly than his contemporaries appreciated.

Born in Ghent, Belgium, Quételet received a doctorate of science from the University of Ghent in 1819. He then taught mathematics in Brussels. Quételet studied astronomy and probability for three months in Paris in 1824. He learned astronomy from François Arago and Alexis Bouvard and the theory of probability from Joseph Fourier and Pierre-Simon Laplace. In 1828, he founded the Royal Observatory of Belgium. He subsequently learned how to run the observatory, giving special attention to its meteorological functions.

One science was not enough, however. Starting around 1830, Quételet became heavily involved in statistics and sociology. More than other scientists of his time, he was convinced that probability influenced the course of human affairs. Astronomers had used the law of error to gain accurate measurement of phenomena in the physical world. Quételet believed the law of error could be applied to human beings. If the phenomena analyzed were part of human nature, Quételet believed that it was possible to determine the average physical and intellectual features of a population. Through gathering the "facts of life," the behavior of individuals could be assessed against how an "average man" would normally behave. Quételet believed it possible to identify the underlying regularities for both normal and abnormal behavior. The "average man" could be known from statistically arraying the facts of life and analyzing the results.

Quételet came to be known as the champion of a new science, dedicated to mapping the normal physical and moral characteristics of societies through statistics; he called it social mechanics. His most influential book was *Sur l'homme et le développement de ses facultés, essai d'une physique sociale* (A treatise on man and the development of his faculties, essay of a social physics), published in 1835. In it, he outlines a project of "social physics" and describes his concept of the "average man" (*l'homme moyen*) who is characterized by the mean values of measured variables that follow a normal distribution. Quételet collected data about many such variables. He thought of "average" physical and mental qualities as real properties of particular people or races and not just abstract concepts. Quételet helped give cognitive strength to ideas of racial differences in 19th-century European thought. His concept of "average man"

...hat it is the central value around which measurements of a human trait are grouped according to a normal bell curve. The "average man" began as a simple way of summarizing some characteristic of a population, but in some of Quételet's later work, he presents average man as an ideal type. He felt that nature intended the average man as a goal, and any deviations from this goal were errors or aberrations. These later ideas were criticized by other scientists—they argued that an average for a population in all dimensions might not even be biologically feasible. What Quételet thought he was measuring might not even exist, in his critics' view.

In 1846, Quételet published a book on probability and social science that contained a diverse collection of human measurements, such as the heights of men conscripted into the French military and the chest circumferences of Scottish soldiers; in many cases the data were approximately distributed. Quételet was among the first to attempt to apply such measurements to social science, incorporated within his proposed "social physics." He was keenly aware of the overwhelming complexity of social phenomena and the many variables that needed measurement. His goal was to understand the statistical laws underlying such phenomena as crime rates, marriage rates, or suicide rates. He wanted to explain the values of these variables by other social factors. In this way, the use of the normal curve, a standard in many sciences such as astronomy but not in the social sciences, had a powerful influence on other scientists, such as Francis Galton and James Clerk Maxwell.

Quételet's study of the statistics of crime and its implications for the populations and races under study prompted questions of free will versus social determinism. These ideas were rather controversial among other contemporary scientists who held that it contradicted a concept of freedom of choice. Were criminals born or made? Were certain populations destined to be criminals, or could people choose to lead an honest life? Quételet's work on the statistics of crime and mortality was used by the government to improve census taking and make policy decisions on issues such as immigration, policing, and welfare.

Quételet also founded several statistical journals and societies, and he was especially interested in creating international cooperation among statisticians. He influenced generations of social scientists in matters of statistics, populations, races, and crime.

CESARE LOMBROSO (1836–1909):
CONTROVERSIAL CRIMINOLOGIST

During the latter part of the 19th century, Cesare Lombroso, an Italian physician who worked in prisons, suggested that criminals have distinctive physical traits. He viewed them as evidence of evolutionary regression to lower forms of human or animal life. To Lombroso, a criminal's "degenerate" physical appearance reflected his or her degenerate mental state, which in turn led to crimes being committed. In 1876, Lombroso theorized that criminals stand out physically, with low foreheads, prominent jaws and cheekbones, protruding ears, hairiness, and unusually long arms. Lombroso felt that all these characteristics made them look like humans' apelike ancestors; therefore, since they were not as developed as modern humans, criminals were lesser humans.

Lombroso's work was flawed, however, since the physical features he attributed to prisoners could be found throughout the entire population. It is now known that no physical attributes, of the kind described by Lombroso, set off criminals from noncriminals.

Many criminals at the time were diagnosed with a disease called *dementia praecox*, which was considered practically incurable. The one who defined the diagnosis was French psychiatrist Bénédict-Augustin Morel in 1860. Morel described a disorder in which the intellectual faculties decompose to an apathetic state resembling dementia. Today this would be recognized as a type of schizophrenia. Morel's work on the "degeneration" of the human species led him to assume that the disposition for mental diseases is passed through family generations, and family members get increasingly more "degenerate" and mentally ill with each generation.

Ten years later, Lombroso adopted Morel's ideas but connected mental diseases and criminality. The ideas of Morel and Lombroso influenced many psychiatrists and academics. For example, the novel *Buddenbrooks* by Thomas Mann, published in German in 1901, is about the decline and fall of a family due to mental illness. The ideas of mental degeneration due to family genetics exerted a disastrous influence on the later development of societies and politics in the United States and Europe, especially Germany.

Lombroso's research was scientifically flawed. Several decades later, Charles Goring, a British psychiatrist, conducted a scientific comparison is tprisoners and people living in society and found no overall physical differences. Today genetics research seeks possible links between biology and crime. Though no conclusive evidence connects criminality to any specific genetic trait, people's overall genetic composition, in combination with social influences, probably accounts for some tendency toward criminality. In other words, biological factors may have a real, but modest, effect on whether or not an individual becomes a criminal.

ALPHONSE BERTILLON (1853–1914): DEVELOPER OF ANTHROPOMETRY

By 1854, efforts were underway in police departments throughout the United States to create local archives of criminal images. The chief difficulty was how to identify habitual thieves (so-called recidivists, or career criminals, as they are called now). As cities grew and the population became more mobile, knowing if people really were who they said they were became increasingly problematic. Judicial sentencing had changed to increase the severity of punishment based on the number and type of crimes committed. Therefore the judges and the police had to know who the criminals were and if they had a record of their past offenses.

Photographs provided a way to catalog recidivists. These included daguerreotype portraits of criminals and "rogues' galleries," which usually comprised photographs placed in racks or assembled into albums. Volumes of mug shots were compiled by local police agencies as well as by private detective organizations such as the Pinkerton National Detective Agency. Volumes containing records of illegal foreigners, for instance the itinerant Chinese population, were probably used for purposes of immigration control. From the 1880s on, identifying details and photographs were commonly featured in the "wanted" posters that were distributed widely to apprehend criminals.

The files developed from this process contained photographs and descriptions of criminals, typically worthless. It was not so much that the descriptions were not accurate—they were as far as that kind of thing goes—it was that there was no *system*. Imagine this: A police clerk has a criminal standing in front of him, and the officer wants to know if they had committed any crimes prior to this one. Now hundreds or possibly thousands of files must be sorted through, in an attempt to recognize the face in front of the clerk from a photograph. Sorting by names does no good; the criminal might be lying. The files cannot be sorted by elements such as beards because the criminal might have shaven to disguise his appearance. For any city of any size, maintaining files became an administrative nightmare. Now think of trying to communicate this information *between* towns and cities with no fax machines, no e-mail, and no Internet. Turning data into accessible information is crucial to making sense of it.

Policemen themselves began to include photographs in albums, either for private record, as in the case of San Francisco policeman Jesse Brown Cook's scrapbooks of that city in the late 19th and early 20th century; or to publicize police activity, as in Thomas Byrnes's *Professional Criminals of America* (1886). Byrnes's book reproduced photographs of mostly "respectable" looking criminals with accompanying comments. Byrnes claimed that, contrary to popular opinion (because of Cesare Lombroso's work), criminals did not necessarily convey the nature of their activities through their physical appearance.

Alphonse Bertillon was the son of anthropometrist Adolphe-Louis Bertillon. Anthropometrics was the science of taxonomy of the human race, which relied on a statistical approach using abstract measurements. Anthropometrics had been used extensively in the colonies by most European powers with colonial interests to study "primitive" peoples. It formed part of the foundation of the modern science of physical anthropology. Bertillon had two traits that defined his life: genius and rebelliousness. He had inherited his father's intelligence, but it was tinged with an unwillingness to suffer those not as bright as he. Bertillon's father had tried to help him with employment but could not help him enough: Alphonse could only find work as a clerk in the Paris police department. The repetitive tasks of filling out and filing forms was mind-numbingly boring to him, and he constantly searched for intellectual outlets.

Bertillon knew from the work of his father and Lombroso that people's characteristics could be measured and that criminals were physically different from "normal" people. Additionally, from the work of Adolphe Quételet, he knew that the measurements of human characteristics tended to fall into statistically relevant groups, but also that no two people should have the same set of measurements. Bertillon surmised that if a record could be made of 11 special measurements of the human body, then that record, when accompanied with a photograph, would establish unique, recordable, systematized identification characteristics for every member of the human race.

Alphonse devised his method and wrote his ideas out as a proposal to Louis Andrieux, the prefect (chief of police). The prefect, a good policeman with little formal education, simply ignored it. Bertillon tried again with another report explaining his method. Andrieux became angry that this clerk was telling him the present system was useless and reprimanded him. Bertillon felt that he was condemned to fill out forms for the rest of his life. His father, however, counseled patience and urged him to continue measuring anyone who would allow it, thus increasing his data. Eventually Andrieux was replaced by a man named Jean Camecasse. Bertillon jumped at this new chance and made his usual presentation. Camecasse was reluctant but gave Bertillon three months to identify at least one career criminal; if he could do that, his method would be adopted.

Bertillon had had two years under Andrieux to accumulate data and perfect his system. The resultant Bertillonage measurements comprised the following 11 elements:

- height
- stretch: length of body from left shoulder to right middle finger when the arm is raised
- "bust": length of torso from head to seat, taken when seated
- length of head: crown to forehead
- width of head: temple to temple
- length of right ear
- length of left foot
- length of left middle finger
- length of left cubit: elbow to tip of middle finger
- width of cheeks (presumably cheekbone)
- length of left little finger

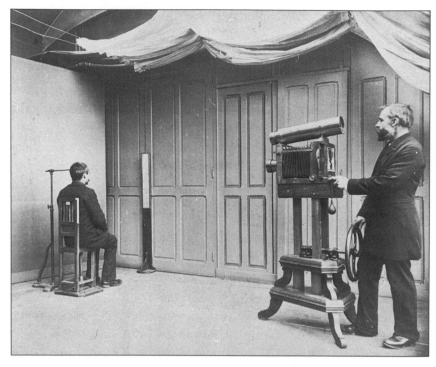

Alphonse Bertillon, a clerk with the Paris police, devised a method of body measurements to effect identification. Bertillon's father was a physical anthropologist who influenced his son's thinking. *(Bridgeman Art Library)*

These measurements were recorded onto a data card, alongside the picture of the criminal and with additional information, such as hair, beard, and eye color. The photographs were taken front and side (the precursor to our modern mug shots). Bertillon called these cards a *portrait parlé*— a spoken portrait that described the criminal both through measurements and words. The "Bertillon card" would then be filed in one of 81 drawers. The drawers were organized by length of head, then by width, then middle fingers, and finally little fingers. On these four measurements, Bertillon could get the odds of identifying any one criminal down to about 1 in 276; after that, the additional measurements would pin him down precisely. The chances of two people having the same measurements were calculated at more than 4 million to one.

Two months and three weeks went by without notice of an identification. Bertillon was a nervous wreck. Near the end of the last week, he processed a criminal named Dupont (his sixth Dupont of the day). After measuring the man, Bertillon sorted through his drawers and cards and found one that matched—the man's name was actually Martin. Bertillon went into the interrogation room and confronted the man with his real identity and arrest record. "Dupont" denied it, but when Bertillon showed the arresting officer the photographs, clearly showing a mole the man had on his face, Martin finally confessed. Bertillon had done it!

Alphonse Bertillon eventually became chief of criminal identification for the Paris police. The Bertillonage system, named after him, became recognized worldwide and was particularly popular in Europe, especially in France. Bertillon standardized the mug shot and the evidence picture and developed what he called *photographie métrique* (metric photography). He intended this system to enable its user to precisely reconstruct the dimension of a particular space and the placement of objects in it, or to measure the object represented. Such pictures documented a crime scene and the potential clues in it prior to its being disturbed in any way. Bertillon used special mats printed with *cadres métriques* (metric frames), which were mounted along the sides of these photographs. Included among these *photographies métriques* are those Bertillon called *photographies stéréometriques* (stereometric photographs), which pictured front and side views of a particular object.

Bertillon's system lasted approximately 20 years. It was abandoned for the same reason it became useful: The archive itself became unwieldy. The Bertillonage apparatus included an overhead camera, under which the subject would recline in two poses for the measurement of stretch and height; plus a camera set up in a precisely measured distance from the subject, for measurement of the facial dimensions, ear, torso, arm, and hand. All these images were photographed against a grided screen, so that the photographs could act as measurement records. Bertillon's equipment was standard photographic equipment with minor modifications, but the system's central instrument was not the camera but the filing cabinet. At some point it became too difficult to record, maintain, and search through tens of thousands of cards.

Beyond the complexity of the system, other issues began to undermine Bertillon's method. First, it was too difficult to get other clerks to conduct Bertillon's measurements exactly the way he wanted them taken. Bertillon was an exacting man, and the difference between a couple of millimeters might keep a criminal from being identified. Second, a new forensic method was gaining ground that would overshadow Bertillonage: fingerprints.

HANS GROSS (1847–1915): CRIMINALISTICS PIONEER

Hans Gross is generally acknowledged as the founder of scientific criminal investigation. The 1893 publication of his landmark book *Handbuch für Untersuchungsrichter* (A handbook for examining magistrates; published in the English language as *Criminal Investigation*) placed science at the forefront of investigating criminal activities. Gross emphasized the use of the microscope in studying trace materials that might show associations between the criminal, the victim, and the crime scene. The handbook also included discussions of forensic medicine, toxicology, serology, and ballistics, as well as topics that had never been discussed before—physics, geology, and botany. Even in 1893, Gross complained about the lack of training and application of microscopy in the beginning of his chapter on that topic.

Advanced though the construction of microscopes is today, and

Hans Gross wrote the first textbook on criminal investigation with a scientific perspective.

much as science can accomplish with this admirable artifact, the criminologist has as yet scarcely drawn on the art of the microscopist. Studies of blood, determination of semen spots, and comparison of hairs is virtually all that the microscopist has to do for the criminologist. Other investigations occur only exceptionally, although there are innumerable cases in which the microscopist could provide vital information and perhaps clarify insoluble problems.

Gross, his work, and his book went on to influence and inspire dozens of investigators and forensic scientists. The handbook set the tone for forensic texts to this day.

EDMUND LOCARD (1877–1966):
THE "SHERLOCK HOLMES OF FRANCE"

The Paris police had been trying to track down a group of counterfeiters who were making false franc coins. Some of the alleged counterfeiters had been arrested, but they refused to talk and reveal their sources. A young police scientist named Edmund Locard heard about the case and asked the inspector in charge to see the mens' clothes. The inspector denied the request, but Locard was persistent and repeated it. Finally, the inspector gave Locard one set of clothing. Locard carefully brushed debris off the clothes, paying special attention to the sleeves and shirt cuffs. He then examined the debris under a microscope. Chemical analysis revealed the presence of tin, antimony, and lead—the exact components of the fake francs. The inspector was so impressed that he used Locard again, and other inspectors also caught on, realizing his value in solving cases.

Locard was fascinated by the microscopic debris found on clothing and other items. He was inspired by the German chemist Liebig, who had contended, "Dust contains in small all the things that surround us." From his studies of microscopic materials, Locard knew that there was nothing organic or inorganic that would not eventually be broken, fractured, or splintered into dust or debris. This debris, indicative by shape, chemistry, or composition of its source, demonstrated the associations evident in our environments. He expounded on this concept in his 1930 article "The Analysis of Dust Traces":

> The task is to find out what the state of the matter was before it passed into the pulverized condition. The powdered form results in the destruction of the original appearance, which in general permits us to determine what objects are through our senses or by the use of our instruments. On the other hand, the transformation does not go so far that the objects are reduced to their ultimate elements, as to molecules or atoms. It follows therefore that the dust still contains distinctive characteristics which permit us to determine its origin.

For example, cat or dog owners know it is not possible to leave the house without dog or cat hair on their clothing. A trained microscopist could determine the following:

- that they were hairs;

- in fact, animal hairs;

- specifically, dog or cat hairs; and

- possibly identify the breed.

It is that last part that creates the most value for criminal investigations. Demonstrating associations between people, places, and things involved in criminal acts is the focus of forensic science. Locard realized that the transfer and persistence of this debris was the key to unraveling the activities of criminals. In a paper published in 1930, he stated the following:

> Yet, upon reflection, one is astonished that it has been necessary to wait until this late day for so simple an idea to be applied as the collecting, in the dust of garments, of the evidence of the objects rubbed against, and the contacts which a suspected person may have undergone. For the microscopic debris that cover our clothes and are the mute witnesses, sure and faithful, of all our movements and of all our encounters.

For years Locard studied the dust and debris from ordinary objects as well as evidence; he cataloged hundreds of samples. The amazing part is that he did this all with a microscope, some chemicals, and a small spectrometer. He refined methodologies outlined in Hans Gross's book *Criminal Investigation,* and he preferred to search clothing by hand rather than scraping or shaking. By 1920, his work was widely recognized, and many others were influenced by his work as well as Gross's text. Georg Popp and August Bruning in Germany and J. C. van Ledden-Hulsebosch in Holland became known for their microscopic forensic wizardry.

PAUL LELAND KIRK (1902–1970): THE FATHER OF MODERN AMERICAN CRIMINALISTICS

The death of Paul Leland Kirk in 1970 brought an end to the brilliant and innovative career of one of the country's most unusual and productive men of science. He achieved distinction and renown in biochemistry, but his interest in applying scientific knowledge and techniques to the field of criminal investigation brought him ultimately to international recognition and made him the dominant figure in the emerging discipline of criminalistics.

Dr. Kirk was associated with the University of California, Berkeley, from the conclusion of his graduate studies in 1927 to his death. The only exception was his involvement with the Manhattan Project during World War II. He first received recognition as a microchemist, bringing to this discipline a talent and artistry that soon made him a leader in the field. His microchemistry found practical application in two areas: tissue culture studies and criminalistics. In both these areas, a common theme is evident. At the time he became interested in them, both were more art than science. Indeed, it is doubtful that he could have involved himself in any endeavor that did not require the careful and intricate manipulation of the artist. It is to his credit that he not only elevated the art but, through creative innovation, helped put both areas on a sounder scientific footing.

If Kirk wished to be remembered for any one thing, it was for his contribution to criminalistics. Indeed, the very term *criminalistics* has come into usage largely through Kirk's efforts, and it was he who established the first academic program in criminalistics in the United States. He brought to the profession an insight and scientific rigor rarely seen before his time.

During the last two decades of Kirk's life, criminalistics occupied the major proportion of his time and energy. He was the prime mover in establishing and preserving the educational program at UC Berkeley, and he advised other institutions about establishing their own programs. In addition to his educational duties, he was active in professional consultation, serving both prosecution and defense. He was also increasingly concerned with problems of the profession. In particular, he wanted to see criminalistics recognized not just as a profession but as a unique scientific discipline; this theme was the keynote of many of his publications.

RALPH TURNER (1917–1994): AN EXPERT WITNESS

Born in Milwaukee, Wisconsin, Ralph Turner received a B.S. degree in chemistry from the University of Wisconsin in 1939 and an M.S. in police administration from the University of Southern California. He also received further education at Boston University Medical School and the Yale Center for Alcohol Studies.

Turner left Kansas City to work at Michigan State University (MSU). In 1949, he became involved in a year-long scientific study of drinking "under field conditions," which involved creating a social setting for four to six volunteers to gather every Friday evening to play cards, talk, and drink at their leisure. The participants then agreed to have their consumption tracked and periodically submitted to alcohol-blood level testing. The National Traffic Safety Council funded this project, and Turner's work paved the way toward the establishment of the substance abuse program at MSU in 1976.

From 1959 through 1961, Turner served as chief police adviser to the Police and Security Services of South Vietnam under the auspices of the MSU Advisory Group. He subsequently served as a Fulbright lecturer at the Central Police College of Taipei, Taiwan, in 1963–64. Appointed by the National Science Council of the Republic of China, Turner returned to the Central Police College to serve as the National Visiting Professor for 1969–70. In addition, he taught short courses around the world, from Guam to Saudi Arabia, and he developed and conducted MSU courses in comparative justice in London, England, from 1970 to 1983.

Outside of the classroom, Turner was an adviser to President Lyndon Johnson's Commission on Law Enforcement and Criminal Justice during 1965–66 (the preparation for the "Drunkenness Taskforce Report"). In 1975, he was one of seven civilian criminology experts selected to assess the firearms evidence for the Los Angeles County Court in the assassination of Robert F. Kennedy. Turner was an expert witness throughout his career, often testifying in criminal and civil court cases related to firearms, crime-scene evidence, and alcohol use. In his police consultant service, he worked on more than 500 cases in the areas of criminalistics, police science, and alcohol problems.

Turner was a member of numerous professional organizations and honor societies and a founding member of the American Academy of Forensic Science. He was recognized for his work in 1978 by the Academy of Criminal Justice Sciences in the presentation of the Bruce Smith Award, becoming only the third person to receive this infrequently given honor. In 1981, he received the MSU Distinguished Faculty Award.

Whether fictional or real, these pioneers in forensic science helped to shape the profession. Some, like Dupin and Holmes, framed the profession through concepts that are now familiar, such as that the most minute amount of evidence can change the course of an investigation. Others, like Locard and Turner, were practitioners who improved the science through new methods and applications. Either way, the field of forensic science is built on the works—real or fictional—of these visionaries.

3

What Is Evidence?

Evidence is critical to a trial: It provides the foundation for the arguments the attorneys plan to offer. Evidence is viewed as the impartial, objective, and, sometimes stubborn information that leads a judge or jury to their conclusions. It can be a complicated thing, and much goes into getting evidence ready before it can go into court.

In a trial, the jury or judge hears the facts or statements of the case to decide the issues; whoever determines guilt or innocence is called the trier of fact, whether it is a judge or jury. During the trial, the trier of fact must decide if the statements made by witnesses are true or not. This is done mainly through the presentation of information or evidence.

Evidence can be defined as information—whether in the form of personal testimony, the language of documents, or the production of material objects—that is given in a legal investigation, and that makes a fact or proposition more or less likely. For example, someone is seen leaving the scene of a homicide with a knife, and it is later shown by scientific examination that blood removed from the knife came from the victim. This could be considered evidence that the accused person committed the homicide. Having the association of the blood to the knife makes the proposition that the accused is the murderer more probable than it would be if the evidence did not exist.

KINDS OF EVIDENCE

Most evidence is *real evidence*—that is, it is generated as a part of the crime and recovered at the scene or at a place where the suspect or victim had been before or after the crime. Hair, fingerprints, paint, blood, and shoeprints are all real evidence. Sometimes, however, items of evidence may be created to augment or explain real evidence. For example, diagrams of hair characteristics, a computer simulation of a crime scene, or a demonstration of bloodstain pattern mechanics may be prepared to help the trier of fact understand complex testimony. Such demonstrative evidence is not generated directly from the incident but is created later. Because it helps explain the significance of real evidence, it does help make a proposition more or less probable and is, therefore, evidence.

Circumstantial evidence is evidence based on inference and not on personal knowledge or observation. Most real evidence (blood, hairs, bullets, fibers, fingerprints) is also circumstantial. People may think that circumstantial evidence is weak—think of television dramas where the attorney says, "We only have a circumstantial case." But unless someone directly witnesses a crime, it is a circumstantial case, and given enough of the right kind of evidence, it could be a strong one. That would be *conclusive evidence*: evidence so strong as to overshadow any other evidence to the contrary.

Another type of helpful evidence is that which differs from but strengthens or confirms other evidence. This is called *corroborating evidence*. As an example, finding fingerprints *and* fibers *and* a bag with money that has matching serial numbers to money stolen from a bank in a suspect's possession would corroborate each other. If the evidence, on the other hand, pointed to someone other than the suspect and therefore indicated his or her innocence, that would be *exculpatory evidence*.

Conflicting evidence, which is irreconcilable evidence that comes from different sources, is to be avoided. This will confuse the issues in the case and hamper the trier of fact from reaching a clear decision. Another kind of unhelpful evidence is that which is discovered as a result of illegally obtained evidence (for example, no proper search warrant, as outlined by the Fourth Amendment of the Constitution), called *tainted evidence,* and is therefore inadmissible because of the primary taint. This is called *derivative evidence.* Finally, *hearsay evidence* is given by a witness who relates not what he or she knows personally, but what others have said. This would be like telling the teacher the reason a friend could not hand in her homework is because she told you her dog ate it. Because it is dependent on the credibility of someone other than the witness, and that person is not testifying, hearsay evidence is routinely not allowed in court.

Not all evidence is of equal value: Some items of evidence have more importance than others. The context of the crime and the type, amount, and quality of the evidence will dictate what can be determined and interpreted. Most of the items in our daily lives are mass-produced, including biological materials (humans have thousands of hairs on their bodies, for example). This puts limits and boundaries for what can be said about the relationships between people, places, and things surrounding a crime.

FORENSIC SCIENCE IS HISTORY

Forensic science is a historical science: The events in question have already occurred and are in the past. Forensic scientists do not view the crime as it occurs (unless they are witnesses); they assist the investigation through the analysis of the physical remains of the criminal activity. Many sciences, such as geology, astronomy, archaeology, paleontology, and evolutionary biology, work in the same way: No data is seen *as it is created,* but only the *remains* of those events are left behind. Scientists who study ancient climates (paleoclimatologists) call these remains *proxy data* because they represent the original data. When someone is given the authority to represent someone else, they are called a proxy.

Many sciences routinely analyze proxy data, although they may not call it that. Archaeologists, for example, analyze cultural artifacts of past civilizations to interpret their activities and practices. Likewise, forensic scientists analyze evidence of past criminal events to interpret the actions of the perpetrator(s) and victim(s), as seen in the following table:

	Forensic Science	Archaeology	Geology
time frame	hours, days, months	hundreds to thousands of years	millions of years
activity level	personal; individual	social; populations	global
proxy data	mass-produced	handmade	natural

Forensic science is a historical science because it reconstructs past events from the physical remnants (proxy data) of those events. In this way, forensic science is similar to other historical sciences such as geology, astronomy, paleontology, and archaeology.

Just as archaeologists must sift through layers of soil and debris to find the few items of interest at an archaeological site, forensic scientists must sort through all of the items at a crime scene (think of all the things in your bedroom, for example) to find the few items of evidence that will help reconstruct the crime. The nature and circumstances of the crime will guide the crime scene investigators and forensic scientists to choose the most relevant evidence and examinations.

But Is It *Forensic* Science?

Many people identify forensic science as "science applied to law," but in truth it is not that simple a definition. If a structural engineer is consulted to determine why a bridge failed, writes a report, testifies once, and then never works on a legal case again, is she a *forensic* engineer? Most people would not think so, but what if they did it three or nine or 21 times in their career? Many forensic scientists do not work at government forensic laboratories, so it cannot be defined that way. At what point does the *application* of science in the legal arena shift to *forensic* science?

Reconstructing events to assist the justice system happens all the time without being forensic science proper. A good example is the case of a Florida dentist who unwittingly passed on his HIV infection to several of his patients. It was reported in 1992 by C. Ou and colleagues in *Science* that a young woman with AIDS had probably contracted her HIV infection during an invasive dental procedure. The dentist had been diagnosed with AIDS in 1986 and continued to practice general dentistry for two more years. The dentist went public for the safety of his patients, requesting that they all be tested for HIV infection. Out of 1,100 people who were tested, seven patients were identified as being HIV-positive.

The HIV virus is genetically flexible and can change its genetic makeup during its life cycle, resulting in a variety of related viral family lines or strains. Investigators used the degree of genetic similarity among the HIV strains in the seven infected patients, along with epidemiological information, to evaluate whether the infections originated with the dentist or were from other sources. The investigators used genetic distance and constructed "family tree" diagrams and amino acid "signature patterns."

Of the seven patients, five had no other identified HIV risk other than visiting the dentist. These five patients were infected with HIV strains that were closely related to those of the dentist's infection; moreover, these strains were different from the strains found in the other two HIV-infected patients and 35 other HIV-infected people in the same geographical area. As the authors of the paper noted:

> In the current investigation, the divergence of HIV sequences within the Florida background population was sufficient to identify strain variation. . . . this investigation demonstrates that detailed analysis of HIV genetic variation is a new and powerful tool for understanding the epidemiology of HIV transmission.

They call it an investigation, they are doing DNA analysis, they are reconstructing the transfer of something from one person to others. Is this *forensic* science?

Do not be confused simply because a science is *historical,* because it uses proxy data to represent past events, or because it uses the same techniques or methods as forensic science. Forensic science is the demonstration of relationships between people, places, and things involved in legal cases through the identification, analysis, and, if possible, individualization of evidence. Because nothing legal is at issue in the dentist "case," it is not forensic. With the increased popularity of forensic science, students and professionals must be cautious about the use of *forensic* as a buzzword in the media and professional publications.

THE BASIS OF EVIDENCE: TRANSFER AND PERSISTENCE

When two items come into contact, information is exchanged. Although this seems pretty simple, it is the central guiding principle of forensic science. Developed by Edmund Locard, it posits that this exchange of information occurs, even if the results may not be identifiable or are too small to be found. The results of such a transfer would be considered as proxy data: not the actual transfer itself, but the remnants of that transaction. Because forensic science demonstrates associations between people, places, and things through the analysis of proxy data, essentially all evidence is transfer evidence. The following is a list of some examples in support of this concept.

Item	Transferred *From* (source)	Transferred *To* (target/location)
drugs	dealer	buyer's pocket or car
bloodstains	victim's body	bedroom wall
alcohol	drinking glass	drunk driver's bloodstream
semen	assailant	victim
ink	writer's pen	stolen check
handwriting	writer's hand/brain	falsified document
fibers	kidnapper's car	victim's jacket
paint chips/smear	vehicle	hit-and-run victim
bullet	shooter's gun	victim's body
striations	barrel of shooter's gun	discharged bullet
imperfections	barrel-cutting tool	shooter's gun's barrel

In a sense, all evidence is transfer evidence in that it has a source and moves or is moved from that source to a target/location. Note that there are levels to various types of evidence, from the fundamental (striations on the barrel-cutting tool) to the specific (the bullet in the victim's body identified by the striations).

The conditions that affect transfer amounts include the following:

- the pressure applied during contact

- the number of contacts (six contacts between two objects should result in more transferred material than one contact)

- how easily the item transfers material (mud transfers more readily than does concrete)

- the form of the evidence (solid/particulate, liquid, or gas/aerosol)

- how much of the item is involved in the contact (a square inch should transfer less than a square yard of the same material)

Evidence that is transferred from a source to a location with no intermediaries is said to have undergone direct transfer; it has transferred from A to B. Indirect transfer involves one or more intermediate objects—the evidence transfers from A to C to B.

Indirect transfer can become complicated and poses potential limits on interpretation. For example, Bob owns two dogs and before he goes to work each day, he pets and scratches them. At work, Bob sits in his desk chair and talks on the phone. Bob gets up to get a cup of coffee. On his return, a colleague is sitting in Bob's desk chair waiting to tell him some news. Bob has experienced a *direct transfer* of his dog's hairs from the dog to his pants. Bob's chair, however, has received an *indirect transfer* of his dogs' hairs—Bob's dogs have never sat in his office desk chair! The colleague who sat in Bob's chair has also experienced an indirect transfer of anything on the chair, except for any fibers originating from the chair's upholstery. How does one interpret finding Bob's dogs' hairs on his colleague if it were not known she had sat in Bob's chair? As can be seen, while direct transfer may be straightforward to interpret, indirect transfers can be complicated and potentially misleading. It may be more accurate to speak of direct and indirect *sources,* referring to whether the originating source of the evidence is the transferring item, but the "transfer" terminology has stuck.

The second part of the transfer process is persistence. Once the evidence transfers, it will remain, or persist, in that location until it further transfers (and potentially is lost), degrades until it is unusable or unrecognizable, or is collected as evidence. How long evidence persists depends on the following:

- what the evidence is (such as hairs, blood, toolmarks, accelerants)

- the location of the evidence

- the environment around the evidence

- time from transfer to collection

- "activity" of or around the evidence location

For example, numerous fiber transfer studies demonstrate that, from the time of transfer with normal activity, after about four hours, 80 percent of the transferred fibers are lost. Transfer and persistence studies with other evidence types have shown similar loss rate.

IDENTITY, CLASS, AND INDIVIDUALIZATION

All things are unique in space and time. No two (or more) objects are absolutely identical. Take, for example, a mass-produced product such as a tennis shoe. Thousands of shoes of a particular type may be produced within one year. To help sell more shoes, the manufacturer's goal is to make them all look and perform the same; consumers demand consistency. This is a help and a hindrance to forensic scientists because it makes it easy to separate one item from another (that red tennis shoe is different from this white one), but these same characteristics make it difficult to separate items with many of the same characteristics (two red tennis shoes). Think about two white tennis shoes that come off the production line one after the next: How do you tell them apart? A person standing on the production line might say "this one" and "that one," but if they were mixed up, they probably could not be sorted again. They would have to be labeled somehow, like numbering them "1" and "2."

Now consider if the two shoes are the same except for color: One is white and one is red. Of course they could be sorted by color, but should they be put in the same category? Compared with a brown dress shoe, the two tennis shoes would have more in common with each other than with the dress shoe. All the shoes, however, are more alike than any of them are compared to, say, a baseball bat. Forensic scientists have developed terminology to clarify the way they communicate about these issues.

Identification is the examination of the chemical and physical properties of an object and using those properties to categorize the object as a member of a group. What is the object made of? What is its color, mass, and/or volume? Examining a white powder, performing one or two analyses, and concluding that it is cocaine is identification. Determining that a small colored chip is automotive paint is identification. Looking at debris from a crime scene and deciding it contains hairs from a black Labrador retriever is identification (of those hairs). All of the characteristics used to identify an object help to refine that object's identity and its membership in various groups. The debris has fibrous objects in it, and that restricts what they could be—most likely hairs or fibers rather than bullets, to use an absurd example. The microscopic characteristics indicate that some of the fibrous objects are hairs, that they are from a dog, and the hairs are most like those from a specific breed of dog. This description places the hairs into a group of objects with similar characteristics, called a *class*. All black Labrador retriever hairs would fall into a class; these belong to a larger class of items called *dog hairs*. Further, all dog hairs can be included in the class of *nonhuman hairs* and, ultimately, into a more inclusive class called *hairs*. Going in the other direction, as the process of identification of evidence becomes more specific, it permits the analyst to classify the evidence into successively smaller classes of objects.

Class is a moveable definition: It may not be necessary to classify the evidence beyond *dog hairs* because human hairs or textile fibers are what is of interest. Although it is possible to define the dog hairs more completely, it may not be necessary to do so in the case at hand. Multiple items can be classified differently, depending on what questions need to be asked. For example, an orange, an apple, a bowling ball, a bowling pin, and a banana could be classified by fruit versus nonfruit, round things

Identification and classification are key concepts in forensic science as they provide an infrastructure for making sense out of what a thing or a part of a thing might be. Unlike biological taxonomy, however, forensic classifications are flexible and relate to what characteristics are needed for sorting. For example, these objects could be classified in a variety of ways, such as food/nonfood, sporting/nonsporting, small/large, organic/inorganic, or even fruit/sporting goods/cosmetic use. An item that is the only member of its class has been individualized. *(BizArt)*

versus nonround things, and organic versus inorganic. Notice that the bowling pin does not fit into either of the classes in the last example because it is made of wood (which is organic) but is painted (which has inorganic components).

Stating that two objects share a class identity may indicate they come from a common source. What is meant by a common source depends on the material in question, the mode of production, and the specificity of the examinations used to classify the object. A couple of examples should demonstrate the potential complexity of what constitutes a common source. Going back to the two white tennis shoes, what is their common source—the factory, the owner, or where they are found? Because shoes come in pairs, finding one at a crime scene and another in the suspect's apartment could be considered useful to the investigation. The forensic examinations would look for characteristics to determine if the two shoes were owned by the same person (the "common source"). If the question centered on identifying the production source of the shoes, then the factory would be the common source.

Another example is fibers found on a body left in a ditch that are determined to be from an automobile. A suspect is developed, and fibers from his car are found to be analytically indistinguishable in all tested traits from the crime-scene fibers. Is the suspect's car the common source? For investigative and legal purposes, the car should be considered as such. But certainly it is not the only car with that carpeting: Other models from that car manufacturer or even other car manufacturers may have used that carpeting, and the carpeting may not be the only product with those fibers. But given the context of the case, it may be reasonable to conclude that the most logical source for the fibers is the suspect's car. If the fibers were found on the body but no suspect was developed, part of the investigation may be to determine who made the fibers and track what products those fibers went into in an effort to find someone who owns that product. In that instance, the common source could be the fiber manufacturer, the carpet manufacturer, or the potential suspect's car, depending on what question is being asked.

If an object can be classified into a group with only one member (itself), it has been individualized. An individualized object has been associated with one, and only one, source: It is unique. The traits that allow for individualization depend, in large part but not exclusively, on the raw materials, manufacturing methods, and history of use. Sometimes, sufficiently increasing class traits can lead toward individualization. For example, forensic scientist John I. Thornton's "Ensembles of Subclass Characteristics in Physical Evidence Examination" article on the classification of firearms evidence is an excellent, if overlooked, treatment of this issue.

INDIVIDUALIZATION OF EVIDENCE

To individualize evidence means to be able to put it into a class of its own. It is the logical extension of the classification of evidence discussed above. If a forensic scientist can discover properties (normally physical) of two pieces of evidence that are unique—that is, they are not possessed by any other members of the class of similar materials—then the evidence is said to have been individualized. An example would be the broken window pane of a burglary case: If the broken pieces of glass found at the crime scene can be fit back to a piece of glass in the burglar's tool kit, for example, then it is reasonable to conclude that those pieces of glass were previously one continuous piece of glass. This conclusion implies that there is no other piece of glass in the entire world that those broken pieces could have come from. Obviously no one has tested these pieces of glass against all of the other, similar broken windows to see if they could fit.

Think about it this way. Take 10 of the same windows and break them. Common sense and experience dictate that each breaking of a window pane would result in different sized and shaped fragments being produced. It would not be reasonable to predict or assume that two breakings would yield exactly the same number and shape of broken pieces. The innumerable variables, such as the force of the blow, the thickness of the window, the microstructure of the glass, the chemical nature of the material, and the direction of the blow, cannot be exactly duplicated, and therefore the number and shapes of the fragments produced are essentially random. The probability of two (or more) breaks exactly duplicating the number and shape of fragments is unknown but generally considered to be zero. In another sense, the shapes of the fragments are not random; broken glass does not look like broken wood, ceramic tile, or plastic. It is easy to identify a shard of broken glass and recognize that it is not a splinter of wood.

KNOWN AND QUESTIONED ITEMS

A motorist strikes a pedestrian with his car and then flees the scene in the vehicle. When the pedestrian's clothing is examined, minute specks and smears of paint are found embedded in the fabric. When the automobile is impounded and examined, fibers are found embedded in an area that clearly has been damaged recently. How is this evidence classified? The paint on the victim's coat is *questioned evidence* because the original source of the paint is not known. Likewise, the fibers found on the damaged area of the car are also questioned items. The colocation of the fibers and damaged area and the wounds/damage and paint smears are indicative of recent contact. When the paint on the clothing is analyzed, it will be compared to paint from the car; this is a known sample because it is known where the sample originated. When the fibers from the car are analyzed, representative fibers from the clothing will be collected for comparisons, which makes them known items as well. Thus, the coat *and* the car are sources of *both* kinds of items, which allows for their reassociation, but it is their *context* that makes them questioned or known.

Back at the scene where the body was found, there are some pieces of yellow, hard, irregularly shaped material. In the lab, the forensic scientist will examine this debris and determine that it is plastic, rather than glass, and further it is polypropylene. This material has now been put in the class of substances that are yellow and made of polypropylene plastic. Further testing may reveal the density, refractive index, hardness, and exact chemical composition of the plastic. This process puts the material into successively smaller classes. It is not just yellow polypropylene plastic but has a certain shape, refractive index, density, hardness, and so forth. In many cases this may be all that is possible with such evidence. The exact source of the evidence has not been determined; it is only known that it could have come from any of a number of places where this material is used—class evidence.

Suppose that the car suspected to be involved in a hit-and-run has a turn-signal lens that is broken, and some of the plastic is missing. The pieces are too small and the edges too indefinite for a physical match. Pieces of this plastic can be tested to determine if it has the same physical and chemical characteristics as the plastic found at the crime scene (color, chemical composition, refractive index, and so on). If so, it could be said that the plastic found at the scene could have come from that broken lens. This is still class evidence because there is nothing unique about these properties that would be different from similar plastic turn-signal lenses on many other cars.

Classes are defined by the number and kind of characteristics used to describe them. As an example, think of the vehicle referred to in the fictitious hit-and-run case. Up until this point, it has been referred to as a car, but what if it was a pickup truck—how would that change things? Even within pickup trucks, differences can easily be drawn based simply on manufacturing locations and days. Following this scheme, the number of trucks could be narrowed down to a very few sold at a particular dealership on a particular day. Classes can be scaled and are context-dependent.

RELATIONSHIPS AND CONTEXT

The relationships between the people, places, and objects involved in crimes are critical to deciding what to examine and how to interpret the results. For example, if a sexual assault occurs and the perpetrator and victim are strangers, more evidence may be relevant than if they live together or are sexual partners. Strangers are not expected to have ever met previously and therefore would have not transferred evidence before the crime. People who live together would have some opportunities to transfer certain types of evidence (head hairs and carpet fibers from the living room, for example) but not others (semen or vaginal secretions). Spouses or sexual partners, being the most intimate relationship of the three examples, would share a good deal more information with the victim.

Stranger-on-stranger crimes beg the question of coincidental associations—that is, two things which previously have never been in contact with each other have items on them that are analytically indistinguishable at a certain class level. Attorneys in cross-examination may ask, "Yes, but could not (insert evidence type here) really have come from *anywhere*? Are not (generic class level evidence) very *common*?" It has been proven for a wide variety of evidence that coincidental matches are extremely rare. The variety of mass-produced goods, consumer choices, economic factors, and other product traits create a nearly infinite combination of comparable characteristics for the items involved in any one situation. Some kinds of evidence, however, are either quite common, such as white cotton fibers, or have few distinguishing characteristics, such as indigo dyed cotton from denim fabric. In a hit-and-run case, however, finding blue denim fibers in the grill of the car involved may be significant if the victim was wearing blue jeans (or even khakis).

It is important to establish the context of the crime and those involved early in the investigation. This sets the stage for what evidence is significant, what methods may be most effective for collection or analysis, and what may be safely ignored. Using context for direction prevents the indiscriminate collection of items that clog the workflow of the forensic science laboratory. Every item collected must be transferred to the laboratory and cataloged—at a minimum—and this takes people and time. Evidence collection based on intelligent decision making, instead of fear of missing something, produces a better result in the laboratory and the courts.

COMPARISON OF EVIDENCE

There are two processes in the analysis of evidence. The first has already been discussed: identification. Recall that identification is the process of discovering physical and chemical characteristics of evidence with an eye toward putting it into progressively smaller classes. The second process is comparison. Comparison is performed in order to attempt to discover the source of evidence and its degree of relatedness to the questioned material. The questioned evidence is compared with objects whose source is known. The goal is to determine whether or not sufficient common physical and/or chemical characteristics between the samples are present. If they do, it can be concluded that an association exists between the questioned and known items. The strength of this association depends on a number of factors, including the following:

- kind of evidence

- intra- and inter-sample variation

- amount of evidence

- location of evidence

- transfer and cross-transfer

- number of different kinds of evidence associated to one or more sources

Individualization occurs when at least one unique characteristic is found to exist in both the known and the questioned samples. Individualization cannot be accomplished by identification alone.

Finding similarities is not enough, however. It is very important that no significant differences exist between the questioned and known items. This bears on the central idea of going from "general to specific" in comparison; a significant difference should stop the comparison process in its tracks. What is a significant difference? The easiest example would be a class characteristic that is *not* shared between the questioned and known items, such as tread designs on shoes or shade differences in fiber color. Sometimes the differences can be small, such as a few millimeters' difference in fiber diameter, or distinct, like the cross-sectional shape of fibers or hair color.

Controls

Controls are materials whose source is known and which are used for comparison with unknown evidence. Controls are often used to determine if a chemical test is performing correctly. They may also be used to determine if a location where evidence may be found is interfering with a chemical or instrumental test. Controls are different from known materials, which are collected to represent a particular thing—a shirt, a chair, a car. Controls are used to test the test *itself.*

There are two types of controls: positive and negative. Consider a case where some red stains are found on the shirt of a suspect in a homicide. The first question that needs to be answered about these stains is: Are they blood? There are a number of tests that can determine if a stain may be blood. Suppose one of these tests is run on some of the stains and the results are *negative.* There are a number of reasons why this might happen:

- The stain is not blood.
- The stain is blood but the reagents used to run the test are of poor quality.
- There is something in the shirt that is interfering with the test.

Before concluding that the stain is not blood, a number of additional steps could be taken. One might be to run a different presumptive test and see if the results change. Another is to run the first test on a sample that is known to be blood and should yield a positive test. This known blood is a positive control: It is a material that is expected to give a positive result with the test reagents and serves to show that the test is working properly. In our case, if the positive control yields a correct result, then it can be presumed that the reagents are working properly and other possibilities for the negative result obtained on the blood-soaked shirt must be considered. It may be proposed that the shirt fibers contain some dye or other material that deactivates the blood test so that it will fail to react with blood. To test this hypothesis, some fibers from the shirt that have absolutely no stains on them have the test run on them. This would be a negative control; the results of the test are expected to come out negative. If the test results are negative as expected, it could still mean that the shirt contains something that interferes with the test. This could only be verified by running a different test on the stain.

If the initial test for blood was done on the stained shirt and came out positive, it should not immediately be assumed that the stain is definitely blood; a sample of the unstained shirt fibers should be tested as a negative control. A negative result here would mean that the positive result on the stain probably means that the stain is blood.

What is the consequence of not running a positive or negative control? If a negative control is not incorporated into the test, a false-positive result may be obtained—that is, it may be concluded that the stain is blood when it is not. This gives rise to what statisticians call a type I error. Type I errors are serious because they can cause a person to be falsely incriminated in a crime.

Failure to run a positive control can cause a false negative result. This can give rise to what is called a type II error. This type of error means that a person may be falsely exonerated from a crime that he or she really did commit. Any error is problematic, but from the criminal justice standpoint, a type II error is less serious than a type I error. It is presumably better to have someone falsely released than falsely accused. Positive and negative controls are usually easy to obtain and should be used to minimize the chance of errors.

ANALYSIS OF EVIDENCE: SOME PRELIMINARY CONSIDERATIONS

Science is a way of examining the world and discovering it. The process of science, the scientific method, is proposing and refining plausible explanations about any unknown situation. It involves asking and answering questions in a formal way and then drawing conclusions from the answers. Science, through its method, has two hallmarks. The first is that the questions asked must be testable. It is not scientific to ponder "How many angels can dance on the head of a pin?" or "Why do ghosts haunt this house?" because a test cannot be constructed to answer either of these questions. The second hallmark is repeatability. Science is a public endeavor, and its results are published for many reasons, the most important of which is for other scientists to review the work and determine if it is sound. If nobody but one individual can make a particular experiment work, it is not science. Other scientists must be able to take the same kind of samples and methods, repeat one's experiments, and get the same results for it to be science.

THE METHOD OF SCIENCE

Interestingly, an important person in the history of science was not even a scientist at all, but a lawyer. Sir Francis Bacon, who rose to be lord chancellor of England during the reign of James I, was the author of *Novum Organum* (1620), a significant philosophical work in which he proposed the first theory of the scientific method. According to Bacon, the scientist should be a disinterested observer of the world with a clear mind, unbiased by preconceptions that might influence the scientist's understanding. This misunderstanding might cause error to infiltrate the scientific data. Given enough observations, patterns of data will emerge, allowing scientists to make both specific statements and generalizations about nature.

This sounds pretty straightforward—but it is wrong. All serious scientific thinkers and philosophers have rejected Bacon's idea that science works through the collection of unbiased observations. Everything in scientific investigation, from the words used to the instrumentation and procedures involved, depends on our preconceived ideas and experience about how the world works. It is impossible to make valid observations about the world without knowing what is worth observing and what is not worth observing. People are constantly filtering their experiences and observations of the world through those things that have already been experienced. Objectivity is impossible for people to achieve.

Another important person in the philosophy of science, Sir Karl Popper, proposed that all science begins with a prejudice, a theory, a hypothesis—in short, an idea with a specific viewpoint. Popper worked from the premise that a theory can never be proved by agreement with observation, but it can be proved wrong by disagreement. The asymmetric, or one-sided, nature of science makes it unique among ways of knowing about the world: Good ideas can be proven wrong to make way for even better ideas. Popper called this aspect of science *falsifiability*—the idea that a proper scientific statement must be capable of being proven false. Popper's view of constant testing to disprove statements biased by the preconceived notions of scientists replaced Bacon's view of the disinterested observer.

Sir Francis Bacon (1561–1626): The Scientific Method

Francis Bacon was born in London and was probably homeschooled. In 1573, at age 12, he entered Trinity College at Cambridge University, where his studies of science brought him to the conclusion that teaching methods (and therefore teachers' conclusions) were erroneous. His reverence for Aristotle conflicted with his dislike of Aristotelian philosophy, which seemed to him barren, disputatious, and wrong in its objectives.

Bacon's publications include his *Essays,* as well as *Colours of Good and Evil* and *Meditationes Sacrae,* all published in 1597, the last containing his famous aphorism "knowledge is power"; *The Proficience* and *Advancement of Learning* in 1605; and *Novum Organum* (The new instrumentality for the acquisition of knowledge, 1620), his best-known work. He is also known for *The New Atlantis,* a utopian novel he wrote in 1627.

Bacon's work was not philosophy or science: It was a way of creating a philosophy. He preferred inductive reasoning to deductive and believed that the thoughtful person should proceed from fact to axiom to law. Bacon saw the fallacies or biases that people held as the limiting factor to knowledge. These tendencies disrupted scientists' ability to be objective. He referred to them as idols; for Bacon, an idol was an image, a fixation of the mind that received veneration but was a fallacy, empty and without substance. In *Novum Organum,* Bacon classified the intellectual fallacies of his time under four idol-headings:

- Idols of the Tribe, which were errors common to human nature: "The human understanding is like a false mirror, which, receiving rays irregularly, distorts and discolors the nature of things by mingling its own nature with it."

However, Popper's ideas do not accurately describe science, either. While it may be impossible to prove a theory true, it is almost just as difficult to prove one false by Popper's methods. The trouble lies in distilling a falsifiable statement from a theory. To do so, additional assumptions that are not covered by the idea or theory itself must always be

- Idols of the Cave, which were errors specific to individuals: "Everyone (besides the errors common to human nature in general) has a cave or den of his own, which refracts and discolors the light of nature, owing either to his own proper and peculiar nature; or to his education and conversation with others; or to the reading of books, and the authority of those whom he esteems and admires. . . . So that the spirit of man (according as it is meted out to different individuals) is in fact a thing variable and full of perturbation, and governed as it were by chance."

- Idols of the Marketplace, which Bacon saw as errors arising from the dealings and associations of words and professions in which "it is by discourse that men associate, and words are imposed according to the apprehension of the vulgar. And therefore the ill and unfit choice of words wonderfully obstructs the understanding."

- Idols of the Theater, which were errors arising from the various dogmas of philosophy, professions, and education: "All the received systems are but so many stage plays, representing worlds of their own creation after an unreal and scenic fashion."

The end of induction is the discovery of forms, the ways in which natural phenomenas occur, and the causes from which they proceed.

Karl Popper (1902–1994): Political Philosopher

Sir Karl Raimund Popper was born in Vienna and educated at the University of Vienna. He earned a Ph.D. in philosophy in 1928 and taught secondary school from 1930 to 1936. In 1934, he published his first book, *Logik der Forschung* (The logic of scientific discovery), in which he put forth his theory of potential falsifiability as the criterion demarcating science from nonscience, thereby criticizing psychologism, naturalism, inductionism, and logical positivism.

In 1937, the rise of Nazism led Popper to emigrate to New Zealand, where he became a lecturer in philosophy at Canterbury University College. In 1946, he moved to England to become reader in logic and scientific method at the London School of Economics, where he was appointed professor in 1949. He was knighted by Queen Elizabeth II in 1965 and elected a fellow of the Royal Society in 1976. He retired from academic life in 1969, though he remained intellectually active until his death in 1994.

Popper coined the term *critical rationalism* to describe his philosophy, in which he argued that scientific theories are abstract in nature and can be tested only indirectly by reference to their implications. He held that scientific theory and human knowledge generally are irreducibly conjectural or hypothetical and are generated by the creative imagination in order to solve problems that have arisen in specific historico-cultural settings. Logically, no number of positive outcomes at the level of experimental testing can confirm a scientific theory, but a single counterexample is logically decisive: It shows the theory, from which the implication is derived, to be false. Popper's account of the logical asymmetry between verification and falsifiability lies at the heart of his philosophy of science. It also inspired him to take falsifiability as his criterion of demarcation between what is and is not genuinely scientific: A theory should be considered scientific if—and only if—it is falsifiable.

Theories that better survive the process of refutation are not more true but, rather, more "fit"—in other words, more applicable to the problem situation at hand. Consequently, just as a species' "biological fit" does not predict continued survival, neither does rigorous testing protect a scientific theory from refutation in the future. Yet since it appears that the engine of biological evolution has produced, over time, adaptive traits equipped to deal with more and more complex problems of survival, likewise the evolution of theories through the scientific method may, in Popper's view, reflect a certain type of progress: toward more and more interesting problems. For Popper, it is in the interplay between the tentative theories (conjectures) and error elimination (refutation) that scientific knowledge advances toward greater and greater problems, in a process very much akin to the interplay between genetic variation and natural selection.

Among Popper's contributions to philosophy is his attempt to answer the philosophical problem of induction. The problem, in basic terms, can be understood by example: Just because the sun has risen every day for as long as anyone can remember does not mean that there is any rational reason to believe it will rise tomorrow. There is no rational way to prove that a pattern will continue in the future just because it has in the past. Popper's reply is characteristic, and it ties in with his criterion of falsifiability. He states that while there is no way to prove that the sun will come up, we can theorize that it will. If it does not come up, then it will be disproved, but since at this moment in time it seems to be consistent with our theory, the theory is not disproved.

The Quine-Duhem thesis argues that it is impossible to test a single hypothesis on its own, since each one comes as part of an environment of theories. Thus, we can only say that the whole package of relevant theories has been collectively falsified, but we cannot conclusively say which element of the package must be replaced. An example of this is supplied by the discovery of the planet Neptune: When the motion of Uranus was found not to match the predictions of Newton's laws, the theory that there were seven planets in the solar system was rejected, rather than Newton's laws themselves. Popper discusses this critique of naïve falsificationism in chapters 3 and 4 of *The Logic of Scientific*

(continues)

(continued)

Discovery. For Popper, theories are accepted or rejected via a sort of "natural selection." Theories that say more about the way things appear are to be preferred over those that do not; the more generally applicable a theory is, the greater its value. Thus, Newton's laws, with their wide general application, are to be preferred over the much more specific "the solar system has seven planets."

Thomas Kuhn's influential book *The Structure of Scientific Revolutions* (1962) argued that scientists work in a series of paradigms; it found little evidence of scientists actually following a falsificationist methodology. Popper's student Imre Lakatos attempted to reconcile Kuhn's work with falsificationism by arguing that science progresses by the falsification of research programs rather than the more specific universal statements of naïve falsificationism. Another of Popper's students, Paul Feyerabend, ultimately rejected any prescriptive methodology and argued that the only universal method characterizing scientific progress was "anything goes."

Popper seems to have anticipated Kuhn's observations. In his 1963 collection *Conjectures and Refutations: The Growth of Scientific Knowledge,* Popper writes the following:

> Science must begin with myths, and with the criticism of myths; neither with the collection of observations, nor with the invention of experiments, but with the critical discussion of myths, and of magical techniques and practices. The scientific tradition is distinguished from the pre-scientific tradition in having two layers. Like the latter, it passes on its theories; but it also passes on a critical attitude towards them. The theories are passed on, not as dogmas, but rather with the challenge to discuss them and improve upon them.

Another objection is that it is not always possible to demonstrate falsehood definitively, especially if one is using statistical criteria to evaluate a null hypothesis. More generally, it is not always clear that if evidence contradicts a hypothesis, this is a sign of flaws in the hypothesis rather than of flaws in the evidence. However, this is a misunderstanding of what Popper's philosophy of science sets out to do. In *The Logic of Scientific Discovery,* rather than proffering a set of instructions that merely need to be followed diligently to achieve science, Popper makes clear his belief that the resolution of conflicts between hypotheses and observations can only be a matter of the collective judgment of scientists, in each individual case.

Popper's falsificationism can be questioned logically by asking about statements such as "there are black holes," which cannot be falsified by any possible observation, yet which seem to be legitimately scientific claims. Similarly, it is not clear how Popper would deal with a statement like "for every metal, there is a temperature at which it will melt," which can be neither confirmed nor falsified by any possible observation, yet which seems to be a valid scientific hypothesis. These examples were pointed out by German scientific philosopher Carl Gustav Hempel. Hempel came to acknowledge that logical positivism's verificationism was untenable, but he argued that falsificationism was equally untenable on logical grounds alone. The simplest response to this is that because Popper described how theories attain, maintain, and lose scientific status, individual consequences of currently accepted scientific theories are scientific in the sense of being part of tentative scientific knowledge, and both of Hempel's examples fall under this category. For instance, atomic theory implies that all metals melt at some temperature. Another example is the claim that faster-than-light travel of information is possible, an unfalsifiable claim that would have been viewed as correct before relativistic physics and is now assumed to be false because the theory implies this. If this theory is later rejected, the issue may become more complex. To put it simply, on this view, falsifying a theory may lead to some of its implications being temporarily of uncertain scientific status, not even supported in a hypothetico-deductive sense.

made. If the statement is shown to be false, it is not known if it was one of the other assumptions or the theory itself that was at fault. This confuses the issue and clouds what the scientist thinks he or she has discovered.

Defining science is difficult. It takes a great deal of hard work to develop a new theory that agrees with the entirety of what is known in any area of science. Popper's idea about falsifiability—that scientists attack a theory at its weakest point—is simply not the way people explore the world. To show that a theory is wrong, it would take too much time, too many resources, and too many people to develop a new theory in any modern science by trying to prove every single assumption inherent in the theory false. It would be impossible!

Thomas Kuhn, a physicist by education and training who later became a historian and philosopher of science, offered a new way of thinking about science. Kuhn wrote that science involves paradigms, which are a consensual understanding of how the world works. Within a given paradigm, scientists add information, ideas, and methods that steadily accumulate and reinforce their understanding of the world. Kuhn called this "normal science."

With time, contradictions and observations that are difficult to explain are encountered but cannot be dealt with under the current paradigm. These difficulties are set aside to be dealt with later, so as not to endanger the status quo of the paradigm. Eventually enough of these difficulties accumulate, and the paradigm can no longer be supported. When this happens, Kuhn maintains, a scientific revolution ensues that dismantles the old paradigm and replaces it with a new paradigm.

Kuhn's main point is that while main points of theories are tested— and some are falsified—the daily business of science is not to overturn its core ideas regularly. Falsifiability is not the only criterion for what science is. If a theory makes novel and unexpected predictions, and those predictions are verified by experiments that reveal new and useful or interesting phenomena, then the chances that the theory is correct are greatly enhanced. However, science does undergo startling changes of perspective that lead to new and, invariably, better ways of understanding the world. Thus, science does not proceed smoothly and incrementally, but it is one of the few areas of human endeavor that is truly progressive. The scientific debate is very different from what happens in a court of law, but just as in law, it is crucial that every idea receives the most vigorous possible advocacy, just in case it might be right.

In the language of science, the particular questions to be tested are called hypotheses. Suppose hairs are found on the bed where a victim has been sexually assaulted. Are the hairs those of the victim, the suspect, or someone else? The hypothesis could be framed as: "There is a significant difference between the questioned hairs and the known hairs from the suspect." Notice that the hypothesis is formed as a neutral statement that can be either proved or disproved.

After the hypothesis has been formed, the forensic scientist seeks to collect data that sheds light on the hypothesis. Known hairs from the suspect are compared with those from the scene and the victim. All relevant data will be collected without regard to whether it favors the hypothesis. Once collected, the data will be carefully examined to determine what value it has in proving or disproving the hypothesis; this is its probative value. If the questioned hairs are analytically indistinguishable from the known hairs, then the hypothesis is rejected. The scientist could then conclude that the questioned hairs could have come from the suspect.

Suppose, however, that most of the data suggests that the suspect is the one that left the hairs there, but there is not enough data to associate the hairs to him. It cannot be said that the hypothesis has been disproved (there are some similarities), but neither can it be said that it has been proved (some differences exist, but are they significant?). Although it would be beneficial to prove unequivocally that someone is or is not the source of evidence, it is not always possible. As has previously been stated, not all evidence can be individualized. The important thing to note here is that evidence analysis proceeds by forming many hypotheses and perhaps rejecting some as the investigation progresses.

Some preliminary questions must be answered before hypotheses are formulated. Is there sufficient material to analyze? If the amount of the evidence is limited, then choices have to be made about which tests to perform and in what order. The general rule is to perform nondestructive tests first because they conserve material. Most jurisdictions also have evidentiary rules that require some evidence to be kept for additional analyses by opposing experts; if the entire sample will be con-

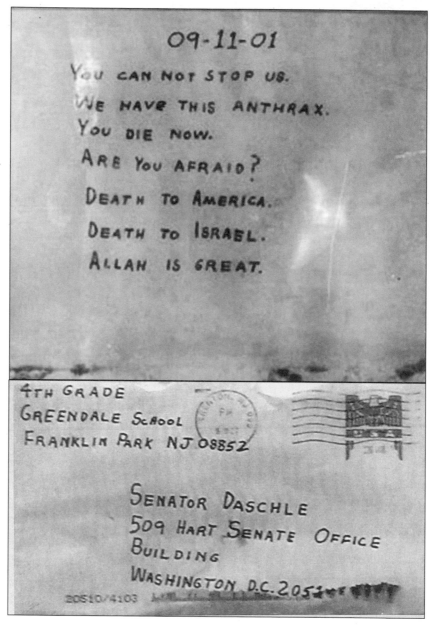

An example of a threatening letter mailed to Senator Tom Daschle in October 2001, which supposedly contained anthrax or some other contagion. Such a letter may be subjected to numerous forensic examinations. *(Associated Press/ Justice Department/FBI file)*

sumed in an analysis, then both sides must be informed that not enough evidence will be available to have additional analyses performed.

If extremely large amounts of material are submitted as evidence, how are they sampled? This often happens in drug cases where, for example, a 50-pound block of marijuana or several kilograms of cocaine are received in one package. The laboratory must have a protocol for sampling large quantities of material so that samples taken are representative of the whole. The other kind of cases where this occurs is where there are many exhibits that appear to contain the same thing—for example, 100 half-ounce packets of white powder. The laboratory and the scientist must decide how many samples to take and what tests to perform. This is especially important because the results of the analyses will ascribe the characteristics of the samples to the whole exhibit, such as identifying a thousand packets of powder as 23 percent cocaine based on analysis of a fraction of the packets.

What happens in cases where more than one kind of analysis must be done on the same item of evidence? Consider a handgun received into evidence from a shooting incident with red stains and possible fingerprints on it. This means that firearms testing, serology, latent print, and possibly DNA analysis must be performed on the handgun. They should be put into an order where one exam does not spoil or preclude the subsequent exam(s). In this case, the order should be first serology, then latent print, and finally firearms testing.

It is important to note that one seemingly small piece of evidence can be subjected to many examinations. Take the example of a threatening letter that supposedly contains anthrax or some other contagion. The envelope and the letter could be subjected to the following:

- disease diagnosis, to determine if it really contains the suspected contagion

- trace evidence, for hairs or fibers in the envelope or stuck to the adhesives (stamp, closure, tape used to seal it)

- DNA, from saliva on the stamp or the envelope closure

- questioned documents, for the paper, lettering, and other aspects of the form of the letter

- ink analysis, to determine what was used to write the message, address, etc.

- handwriting, typewriter, or printer analysis, as appropriate

- latent fingerprints

- content analysis, to evaluate the nature of the writer's intent and other investigative clues

In this example, the ordering of the exams is crucial to ensure not only the integrity of the evidence but also the safety of the scientists and their coworkers. Other evidence can also be very extensive. It is important to realize that *anything* can become evidence, and forensic scientists must keep open minds if they are to solve the most difficult of crimes.

4

Microscopy

The microscope is a nearly universal symbol of science, representing our ability to explore the world below the limits of our perception. Forensic science is equally well-represented by the microscope; illustrations in Sir Arthur Conan Doyle's Sherlock Holmes stories show the great detective peering through a microscope at some minute evidence. As Dr. Peter DeForest, a noted forensic microscopist, has stated, "Good criminalistic technique demands the effective use of the microscope."

The microscope may seem to be a relic of an antiquated age of science when compared with some of today's advanced instrumentation. But as the life's work of Dr. Walter McCrone and others has shown, microscopy is applicable to every area of forensic science. Microscopy can be as powerful as many current technologies, and in some cases more powerful. For example, microscopy can easily distinguish between cotton and rayon textile fibers, whereas to an infrared spectrometer they both appear to be cellulose. The following table is a list of materials that benefit from microscopy.

A SELECTED LIST OF MATERIALS IN MICROSCOPY APPLICATION IN FORENSIC SCIENCE

art forgeries	asbestos	building materials
bullets	chemistry	drugs
dust	fibers	fingerprints
food poisoning	glass	hairs
handwriting	minerals	paint
paper	photographic analysis	pollen
polymers	product tampering	questioned documents
serology	soil	tapes
toolmarks	wood	

Forensic microscopy is more than simply looking at small things. It requires the student (and the expert) to know a great deal about many things, how they are made, how they are used, and their physical and chemical natures. Emile Chamot and Clyde Mason, in their classic *Handbook of Chemical Microscopy, Volume 1,* (1983) succinctly describe the role of the forensic (or technical, in their words) microscopist as follows:

The technical microscopist is concerned with form, but also with formation and function. He needs to know, as completely as possible, the existing structure of the specimen, but he frequently has to investigate or at least postulate how that structure developed or was produced, how it can be controlled, and how it affects performance. The correlation of these three aspects of his studies is too specific to the material involved to be dealt with here. . . . But even descriptive microscopy often requires more than superficial observation, or the ordinary arts of varying focus and illumination that experience makes habitual. And there are many properties closely governing non-microscopical behavior that can be usefully explored, as a background for understanding it and as an adjunct to tests on a larger scale.

A full explanation of microscopy and the optical principles involved is beyond the scope of this book—the physics and geometry can get complicated. For this book we will discuss the basics necessary to understand the analysis of hairs and fibers. A list of additional sources can be found in the appendix.

MAGNIFICATION SYSTEMS

If more detail is needed in studying an object—a postage stamp, for example—we need to magnify the image. The easiest way to do this is with a common pocket magnifier or hand lens; this is a simple magnification system, a single lens used to form an enlarged image of an object. A similar system is used to project the image of a 35 mm slide or transparency in a lecture hall. If the screen where the focused image is projected is removed and replaced by a hand lens, a larger image would be projected. This is the basic principle of all microscopy—a compound magnification system where magnification occurs in two stages and the total magnification is the product of the first lens and the second lens. The observer looks at the first image with a lens that produces an enlarged image called a virtual image. This is the image the eye perceives—a real, projectable image does not exist where the virtual image appears to be—and is visible only as a result of the compound magnification system. A more commonplace example of a virtual image

With one lens, an object can only be magnified so far; an additional lens is required to increase the size of the first image. *(Courtesy of the author)*

Walter McCrone (1916–2002): A Preeminent Microscopist

Dr. Walter Cox McCrone was an American chemist who was considered one of the leading experts in microscopy. McCrone received a bachelor's degree in chemistry from Cornell University in 1938 and a Ph.D. in organic chemistry from the same institution in 1942. He became a microscopist and materials scientist at the Armour Research Foundation (now the Illinois Institute of Technology) from 1944 to 1956 after a two-year postdoctoral position at Cornell. McCrone left his job in 1956 to become an independent consultant. In 1960, he founded McCrone Associates (part of the McCrone Group), an analytical consulting firm in Chicago, Illinois (now located in Westmont, Illinois). That same year, he founded the McCrone Research Institute, a nonprofit organization for teaching and research in microscopy and crystallography. Since its beginning, the institute has taught more than 25,000 students in all facets of microscopy. The McCrone Research Institute remains a leading educational facility within the world of microscopy. In the 1990s, Dr. McCrone and his wife Lucy endowed a chair of chemical microscopy in the College of Arts and Sciences at Cornell. Named the Emile M. Chamot Professorship in Chemistry, it honors Emile Monnin Chamot, a Cornell professor of chemical microscopy.

McCrone was a prodigious researcher, authoring and coauthoring more than 600 technical articles and 16 books or chapters. He was instrumental in promoting the use of microscopy to chemists. *The Particle Atlas,* his best-known publication, written with other McCrone Associates staff members, appeared as a single volume in 1970 and as a six-volume second edition in 1973. Today it is available on CD-ROM and is still recognized as one of the best handbooks available for solving materials analysis problems. For 30 years, McCrone edited and published *The Microscope,* an international quarterly journal of microscopy that was started by Arthur Barron in 1937 and is dedicated to the advancement of all forms of microscopy for the biologist, mineralogist, metallographer, forensic scientist, and chemist. *The Microscope* publishes original works from the microscopical community and serves as the proceedings of the Inter/Micro microscopy symposium held annually in Chicago.

McCrone's most famous analytical work was his participation in the Shroud of Turin Research Project (STURP). The Shroud of Turin is a length of linen cloth purported to be the burial shroud of Jesus. In 1977, a team of scientists selected by the Holy Shroud Guild—proponents of the shroud's authenticity—proposed a series of tests to determine the shroud's origins. The archbishop of Turin granted permission, and the STURP scientists conducted their testing over five days in 1978. McCrone, upon analyzing the samples he had, concluded that the red stains that had been pointed to as blood were actually pigment—specifically, red ochre and vermilion tempera paint. Two others on the STURP team published their own peer-reviewed analysis, which concluded that the stains were blood. Neither team member was a forensic serologist or a pigment expert. Later presentations at scientific meetings explained how results similar to theirs could be obtained from tempera paint. McCrone adhered to his opinion that comparison of microscopic images showed that the stain on the shroud was not blood.

McCrone resigned from the STURP team in June 1980. Until his death in 2002, he continued to comment on and explain the analysis he had performed, and he became a prominent figure in the ongoing Shroud of Turin controversy. *Judgment Day for the Shroud of Turin,* his book on the subject, was published in 1999. McCrone's contentious conclusion that the Turin shroud is a medieval painting was subsequently vindicated by carbon-14 dating in 1988. In 2000, he received the American Chemical Society National Award in Analytical Chemistry for his work on the Turin shroud and for his tireless patience in the defense of his work for nearly 20 years.

is that seen in a mirror: Standing 2 inches (5.1 cm) away from the mirror, our image in the mirror looks as if it is standing 2 inches (5.1 cm) away from the other side of the mirror. If a white screen or glass plate were substituted for the mirror, no image would be visible. By contrast, a real image is one that can be seen *on* the screen—that is, projected *onto* the screen.

THE LENS

Most people are familiar with the lens in their daily lives as eyeglasses, reading magnifiers, contact lenses, and the like. In microscopy, a lens means a very specific thing: a translucent material that bends light in a known and predictable manner. For example, an ideal converging lens causes all light entering the lens from one side to meet again at a point on the other side of the lens. In doing so, an image of the original object is produced.

The size and position of an image produced by a lens can be determined through geometry based on the lens's focal length, which is the distance between the two points of focus on either side of the lens. Focal

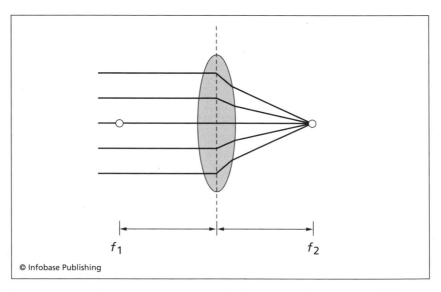

© Infobase Publishing

In microscopy, a lens means a very specific thing; a translucent material that bends light in a known and predictable manner.

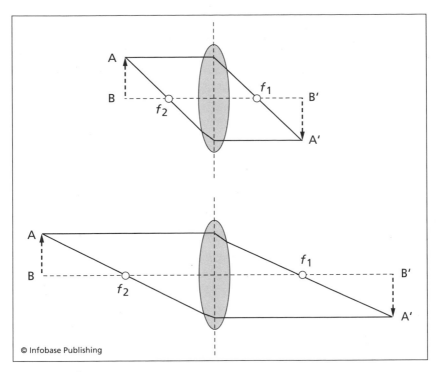

Focal length, the distance between the two points of focus on either side of a lens, is important in microscopy because it determines much of the image quality.

length is important in microscopy because it determines much of the image quality. Think of it this way: If one eye is too far or too close, a clear image of an object is difficult to see. Why? Human eyes, being curved, cannot maintain a clear point of focus for all distances: About 10 inches (25 cm) is the distance that a human eye can easily distinguish between two objects next to each other. Lenses are made using this "ideal" viewing distance, or focal length.

At 10 inches (25 cm), the resolution, or the minimum distance between two objects, can be separated, and the objects can be distinguished; by the human eye, it is only between 0.15 and 0.30 mm. Therefore, this is the limit of our eyes without assistance; if better resolution (that is, to see more detail in the postage stamp) is required, the image must be magnified. If a hand lens magnifies an image four times (the shorthand for this is "4×"), then two objects that are about

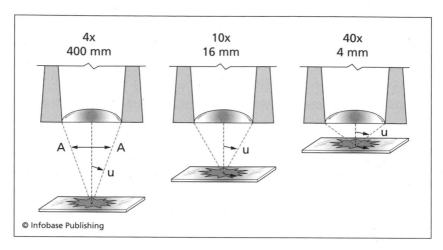

Numerical aperture is a measure of the light-gathering ability of a lens. It is a central trait in the quality of a lens.

0.05 mm apart can be resolved. Magnification with one lens cannot continue indefinitely, however. As magnification *increases,* lens diameter *decreases* to bend the light more to make a larger image. A simple lens that magnifies 1,000× would be only 0.12 mm in diameter! Therefore, about 10×–15× is the practical limit of magnification for simple lenses.

COMPOUND MAGNIFYING SYSTEMS

A compound microscope, as the name implies, employs a magnification system to exceed the limits imposed on simple lenses. A second lens is placed in line with the first lens, and this further enlarges the image. The total magnification of the microscope is the product of the two lenses. A 10× lens and a 4× lens would produce a 40× image (10 × 4 = 40), or one that has been magnified 40 times. Lenses of up to 30× can be used in a compound microscope.

Even lenses in compound microscopes have resolution limits, however, and it is possible to continue to magnify an image but not improve its resolution; this is called *empty magnification.* The result of empty magnification is a larger but fuzzier-looking image.

THE MICROSCOPE

The fundamental design of the microscope has not changed much since its original invention; improvements to nearly every component, however, have made even the most inexpensive microscopes suitable for basic applications. The text in this section refers to the diagram of the parts of a simple microscope.

Starting at the top, the eyepiece, or ocular, is the lens that is looked through when viewing an object microscopically. A microscope may be monocular, having one eyepiece, or binocular, having two eyepieces; most microscopes found in laboratories today are binocular. Typically the eyepiece(s) will have a magnification of 10× and may be focusable; this provides the viewer to adjust the eyepieces if one eye is stronger than the other. The area seen when looking through the eyepieces is called the field of view and will change if the specimen is moved or the magnification is changed.

The next lens in the microscope is called the objective lens (or just "the objective") because it is closest to the object or specimen being studied. The objective is the most important part of the microscope. Objectives come in many types and magnifications (typically 4×, 10×, 15×, 20×, and 25×). Each objective will have information about it engraved into its body in a specific format. Although the information may vary by manufacturer, an objective will usually have the magnification,

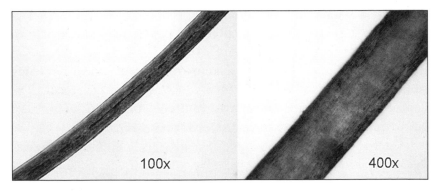

Increased magnification does not always yield a better image. At some point, all that is left is a larger but blurry image; this is called empty magnification. *(Courtesy of the author)*

numerical aperture, tube length, and thickness of coverslip that should be used with it. The numerical aperture is an angular measure of the lens's light-gathering ability and, ultimately, its resolving quality. The tube length is the distance from the lowest part of the objective to the upper edge of the eyepiece; this has been standardized at 160 mm in modern microscopes. Because the tube length determines where the in-focus image will appear, the objectives must be designed and constructed for a specific tube length. Coverslips, the thin glass plates that are placed on top of mounted specimens, protect the specimen and the objective from damage. They come in a range of thicknesses measured in millimeters (0.17 mm, for example). All of this information is important to the microscopist's proper use of a particular objective.

Achromatic objectives are the least expensive objectives and are found on most microscopes. These objectives are designed to be corrected for chromatic aberration, where white light from the specimen is broken out into multiple colored images at various distances from the lens. Achromats are corrected for red and blue only, and this can lead to substantial artifacts, such as colored halos. Because of this, it may be necessary to use a green filter and employ black and white film for photomicrography.

A simple lens focuses a flat specimen on a microscope slide onto the lens, a rounded surface. This results in an aberration called curvature of field and results in only part of the image being in focus. Regular apochromats lack correction for flatness of field, but recently most manufacturers have started offering flat-field corrections for achromat objectives, called plan achromats.

Astigmatism, or spherical aberration, results from a lens not being properly spherical. When this happens, specimen images seem to be "pulled" in one direction when focusing through the lens. Most modern microscope objectives are corrected for spherical aberration.

A step up in corrected lenses is called fluorites, or semi-apochromats, because the mineral fluorite was the original method used for correction. Fluorites are also corrected for spherical aberration, where the light passing near the center of the lens is less refracted than the light at the edge of the lens. Fluorite objectives are now made with advanced glass formulations that contain fluorspar or synthetic substitutes. These materials give fluorites a higher numerical aperture, better resolution, and higher contrast. The cost for fluorite objectives, of course, is higher than that for achromats.

The most highly corrected objectives are the apochromats, which contain several internal lenses that have different thicknesses and curvatures in a specific configuration unique to apochromats. Apochromats are corrected for three colors (red, green, and blue) and thus have almost no chromatic aberration. They are very costly but provide even better numerical aperture and resolution than fluorites.

In the last decade, major microscope manufacturers have all migrated to infinity-corrected lens systems. In a typical microscope, the tube length (distance from the top of the eyepiece to the bottom of the objective) is set to 160 mm, but in the newer systems, the image distance is set to infinity, and a lens is placed within the tube between the objective and the eyepieces to produce the intermediate image. Infinity-corrected lens systems produce very-high-quality images and allow for the addition of a variety of analytical components to the microscope. More information on infinity-corrected lenses and microscopy can be found at www.microscopyu.com, a Web site that is designed to provide an educational forum for all aspects of optical microscopy, digital imaging, and photomicrography.

In the intricate card game of microscopy, numerical aperture always trumps magnification. The minimum distance d which must exist between two separate points in the specimen in order for them to be seen as two distinct points is:

$$d = \lambda/2NA$$

or the wavelength of light divided by twice the numerical aperture (NA). The NA is further defined as:

$$NA = n \sin u$$

where n represents the refractive index of the medium between the cover slip and the front lens, and u is half the angle of aperture of the objective. The refractive index of air is 1.0; practically speaking, this means the NA of any lens system with air as the intermediate medium (so-called dry systems; other systems use oil as the intermediate medium, improving their NA) will be less than 1 because half of the angle u in air cannot be more than 90°.

The resolving power of the human eye or the objective lens is not enough for a magnification of, say, 10,000×, because two points on the object can only be seen as separate if the distance between them is within the limit of the resolving power. If the distance is below the resolving power, then two objects would not be seen; if it were higher, only two (and not several) points with no more detail than before would be seen. The maximum magnification available is about 1,000 times the NA of the objective.

The microscope stage is the platform where the specimen sits during viewing. The stage can be moved up or down to focus the specimen image, meaning that portion of the specimen in the field of view is sitting in the same horizontal plane; typically, stages are equipped with a coarse and fine focus. Stages may be mechanical (that is, having knobs for control of movement), rotating (able to spin in 360° but not move back and forth), or both.

August Köhler (1866–1948): Köhler Illumination

August Köhler was a professor and staff member of Zeiss Optical Works in Jena, Germany, best known for his development of the microscopy technique of Köhler illumination. This method optimized microscopical resolution by evenly illuminating the specimen and the field of view. Köhler's invention revolutionized microscope design and is still used in modern digital-imaging techniques.

Köhler studied at the universities in Heidelberg and Giessen. He graduated in 1888 and taught at various schools before returning to university. He learned from and taught for Professor J. W. Spengel at the Institute of Zoology at the University of Giessen, Germany, where he received a doctorate in 1893. In his doctoral research, he primarily pursued microscopy and continually worked to improve the quality of photographs taken through the microscope. He was invited to join Zeiss Optical Works in 1900 because of his earlier work on microscope illumination. He worked for Zeiss for 45 years and was central to the development of microscope design. Köhler was professor for photomicrography (taking photographs through a microscope) at the University of Jena from 1922 until he retired in June 1945.

The condenser is used to obtain a bright, even field of view and improve image resolution. Condensers are lenses below the stage that focus or condense the light onto the specimen field of view. Condensers also have their own condenser diaphragm control to eliminate excess light and adjust for contrast in the image. The condenser diaphragm is different from the field diaphragm, a control that allows more or less light into the lens system of the microscope.

The illumination of the microscope is critical to a quality image and is more complicated than merely turning on a lightbulb. Two main types of illumination are used in microscopy: critical and Köhler. Critical illumination concentrates the light on the specimen with the condenser lens; this produces an intense lighting that highlights edges but may be uneven. Köhler illumination, named after the German microscopist August Köhler in 1893, sets the light rays parallel throughout the lens system, allowing them to evenly illuminate the specimen.

When Köhler was a graduate student, microscopes were illuminated by gas lamps, mirrors, or other primitive light sources. These light sources resulted in uneven specimen illumination, and this produced poor-quality photomicrographs. In his graduate work, Köhler developed an illumination configuration that evenly illuminated the field of view while reducing glare. He added a collector lens for the lamp that focused the light source on the front aperture of the condenser, which could then be focused on the specimen. This superior illumination scheme is still widely used in modern microscopes and forms the basis for many analytical microscopical methods.

Köhler's groundbreaking work on microscope illumination was published in the *Zeitschrift für wissenschaftliche Mikroskopie* in 1893 in Germany, followed by "A New System of Illumination for Photomicrographic Purposes," an English translation of his work in the *Journal of the Royal Microscopical Society* one year later. Today the Köhler illumination is considered one of the most important principles in achieving the best optical resolution on a light microscope.

Köhler illumination is considered the standard set-up for microscopic illumination.

REFRACTIVE INDEX

The refraction of visible light is an important characteristic of lenses that allows them to focus a beam of light onto a single point. Refraction (or bending of the light) occurs as light passes from one medium to another when there is a difference in the index of refraction between the two materials. It is responsible for a variety of familiar phenomena such as the apparent distortion of objects partially submerged in water.

Refractive index is defined as the relative speed at which light moves through a material with respect to its speed in a vacuum. By convention, the refractive index of a vacuum is defined as having a value of 1.0. The index of refraction, N, of other transparent materials is defined through the following equation:

$$N = C / V$$

where C is the speed of light and V is the velocity of light in that material. Because the refractive index of a vacuum is defined as 1.0 and a vacuum is devoid of any material, the refractive indexes of all transparent materials are therefore greater than 1.0. For most practical purposes, the refractive index of light through air (1.0003) can be used to calculate refractive indexes of unknown materials. Refractive indexes of some common materials are shown in the following table.

REFRACTIVE INDEXES OF SEVERAL KNOWN MATERIALS

Material	Refractive Index
air	1.0003
ice	1.310
water	1.330
glass, soda-lime	1.510
ruby	1.760
diamond	2.417

When light passes from a less dense medium (such as air) to a denser medium (such as water), the speed of the wave decreases. Alternatively, when light passes from a denser medium (water) to a less dense medium (air), the speed of the wave increases. The angle of refracted light is dependent on both the angle of incidence and the composition of the material into which it is entering. The "normal" is defined as a line perpendicular to the boundary between two substances. Light will pass into the boundary at an angle to the surface and will be refracted according to Snell's Law:

$$N_1 \times \sin(q_1) = N_2 \times \sin(q_2)$$

where N represents the refractive indexes of material 1, and material 2 and q are the angles of light traveling through these materials with respect to the normal. There are several important points that can be

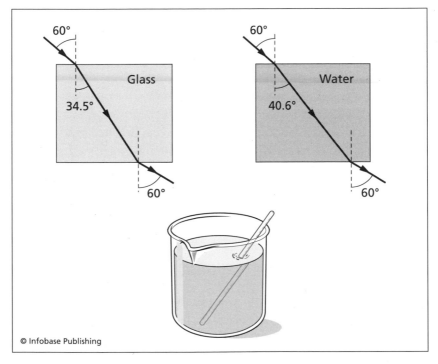

© Infobase Publishing

The ratio of the speed of light in a vacuum and the speed of light in a material is called *refractive index*. In a sense, it is the "optical density" of the material and indicates how much denser that substance is than a vacuum.

drawn from this equation. When $N_{(1)}$ is greater than $N_{(2)}$, the angle of refraction is always smaller than the angle of incidence. Alternatively, when $N_{(2)}$ is greater than $N_{(1)}$ the angle of refraction is always greater than the angle of incidence. When the two refractive indexes are equal ($N_1 = N_2$), then the light is passed through without refraction. The concept of refractive index is illustrated on page 85 for the case of light passing from air through both glass and water. Notice that while both beams enter the denser material through the same angle of incidence with respect to the normal (60°), the refraction for glass is almost 6° more than that for water due to the higher refractive index of glass.

Samples to be viewed in transmitted light must be in a material with a refractive index that is close to their own index. Numerous materials are commercially available to use as mounting media or mountants. The refractive index of water is about 1.33 and therefore makes a poor mountant because it refracts the light so much less than a hair, which has a refractive index of about 1.5 or so.

USING MICROSCOPY AND DOG HAIRS TO CATCH A KILLER

In the early hours of August 17, 1994, the partially burned and battered bodies of a man and a woman were discovered in what remained of their home. A witness later told detectives that he saw a person, accompanied by a dark, medium-sized dog, running away from the property shortly before the fire started. An inspection of the property immediately revealed that Ben, the couple's Australian cattle dog, was missing. He was found days later, six miles from the home. The murdered couple were identified as Jeremy Torrens and Karen Molloy (all names have been changed). The fire and smoke had practically obliterated all chances of finding any evidence that may have linked the murderer to the scene of the crime.

Dennis Molloy, Karen's son, was interviewed and gave conflicting accounts not only on his movements of that night but also on his last contact with the couple and the dog. He claimed to be six miles (9.7 km) away from the couple's home on that night, yet he was seen on a service station's security camera only two miles (3.2 km) from the home just 45 minutes before the fire. He also claimed that he had not had contact with Ben for months before the murders, and yet hundreds of animal hairs were found on and around his bed, on the inside of his car, and on one of his sweatshirts. A witness's statement led investigators to believe that the suspect was someone with whom Ben was familiar because he was never heard barking. Typically Ben was aggressive toward strangers and protective of his owners.

Investigators focused on the hairs found on Dennis Molloy's belongings. The large number of hairs suggested an association of his environment with an animal, a finding that challenged his repeated denials that any animal, including Ben, had been in contact with his belongings. The forensic examination of some 400 animal hairs was challenging. The following two propositions needed to be considered:

Were the hairs those of a dog?
    If the hairs originated from a dog, could that dog have been an Australian cattle dog like Ben, or could they have come from another breed?

Were the questioned hairs transferred as a result of a direct source or an indirect source?
    A direct source is one that has transferred material from the originating source; an indirect source has its material transferred through an intermediary.

Hairs are a particular structure common only to mammals: They are the fibrous growths that originate from their skin. Other animals have structures that may appear to be or are even called hairs, but they are not. A hair is a complicated, composite material with many intricately organized structures, only some of which are visible under the microscope. A single hair on a macroscale has a root, a shaft, and a tip. The root is the portion that formerly was in the follicle, the most proximal (the direction toward the body) portion of the hair. The shaft is the main portion of the hair. The tip is the most distal (the direction away from the body) portion of the hair.

Internally, hairs have a variable and complex microanatomy. The three main structural elements in a hair are the cuticle, the cortex, and the medulla. The cuticle of a hair is a series of overlapping layers of scales that form a protective covering. Animal hairs have scale patterns that vary by species, and these patterns are a useful diagnostic tool for identifying them as animal hairs. Humans have a scale pattern called imbricate, but it is fairly common among animals, and despite attempts to use scales as an individualizing tool for human hairs, it is not generally useful in forensic examinations.

The next structure is the cortex, which makes up the bulk of the hair. The cortex consists of spindle-shaped cells that contain or constrain numerous other structures. Pigment granules are found in and dispersed variably throughout the cortex. The granules vary in size, shape, aggregation, and distribution—all excellent characteristics for forensic comparisons. Small bubbles, called cortical fusi, may appear in the cortex; when they do appear, they may be sparse, aggregated, or evenly distributed throughout the cortex. Cortical fusi also vary in size and shape.

First of all, animals have three types of hairs. *Guard hairs* are large, stiff hairs that make up the outer part of the animal's coat; they are the hairs that should be used for microscopic identification. Guard hairs may have a widening in the upper half of the shaft, called a shield. Below the shield, if it is present, may often be found a subshield stricture, a narrowing of the hair to slightly less than the normal, nonshield shaft diameter. A subshield stricture may be accompanied by a bend in the shaft at the stricture.

Thinner, softer fur hairs fill in the rest of the coat, providing warmth and bulk. Fur hairs are generic in their appearance and are typically useless for microscopic identification. The root may give an indication as to taxonomic origin, but it may also be misleading; it is best not to use fur hairs for microscopic evaluations.

Finally, animals have *vibrissa,* the technical term for whiskers, the short-to-long, stiff, often white hairs around the snout and muzzle. No comprehensive study has been made on the identification of taxonomic origin by vibrissa, probably because these hairs have a long life cycle and are lost comparatively less often than the myriad guard and fur hairs of a typical animal.

Some nonhuman hairs are color-banded, showing abrupt color transitions along the shaft of the hair, including the tip. Raccoons, for example, have four color bands in their guard hairs; incidentally, they are the only animals known to have this many bands.

The hairs in the Molloy case were initially examined to confirm animal origin. The examination showed that several hairs exhibited two colors along the shaft, sometimes three, the color changes being very abrupt and pronounced. This banding does not occur in human hairs. In addition, examining the roots using a low-power microscope, with 10–50× magnification, revealed that the roots of the hairs were large and elongated, unlike human hairs, whose roots are indistinct and round in comparison. Animal origin was established, and further analysis was done to show likely species of origin. The roots, scale pattern, and medullary index were examined and proved that the hairs were likely to have come from a dog. Samples were collected from a variety of sources to determine whether the hairs were those of an Australian cattle dog. Using a comparison microscope with up to 400× magnification, known samples from Ben, and questioned samples, it was shown that the hairs were consistent with each other. Based on the examiner's experience and the quantity of hair in the locations, she determined that the hair was a result of primary transfer. Molloy was found guilty of murder.

The lack of physical evidence in this case forced investigators to look at circumstantial hair evidence, which implicated Dennis Molloy in the homicides. The hairs were useful because of the knowledge and experience of investigators in recognizing, collecting, and examining the hairs as important pieces of evidence both visually and microscopically.

POLARIZED LIGHT MICROSCOPY

One of the most powerful tools forensic scientists have at their disposal is the polarized light microscope (PLM), a tool of nearly infinite uses and applications. Sadly, in this age of computerized instrumentation, few scientists routinely use a PLM, even if they know how. Something can be learned about almost every kind of sample, from asbestos to zircon, by using a PLM. The microscope exploits optical properties of materials to discover details about the structure and composition of materials, and these lead to its identification and characterization.

Materials fall into one of two categories. The first are materials that demonstrate the same optical properties in all directions, such as gases, liquids, and certain glasses and crystals. These are *isotropic materials*. Because they are optically the same in all directions, they have only one refractive index. Light therefore passes through them at the same speed with no directional restrictions.

The second category is *anisotropic materials,* which have optical properties that vary with the orientation of the incoming light and the optical structure of the material. About 90 percent of all solid materials are anisotropic. The refractive indexes vary in anisotropic materials depending both on the direction of the incident light and on the optical structure. Think of anisotropic materials as having a "grain," like wood, with preferential orientations.

Because of their inhomogeneous internal structure, anisotropic materials divide light rays into two parts. A PLM uses this to cause the light rays to interact in a way that yields information about the material. Light is emitted from a source in all directions; in the wave model of light, all directions of vibration are equally possible. If the light passes through a special filter, called a polarizer, then the only light that passes is that which vibrates in the "preferred" direction. Our eyes are "blind" to vibration direction of light; it can be seen only by a color effect or by intensity. This may sound complicated, but chances are good that most of us have seen polarized light—through polarized sunglasses! They reduce the glare, such as the sun shining off a car hood on a bright day, by filtering out all the light except for that which

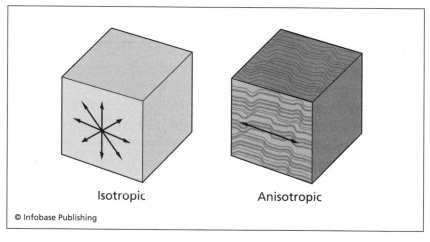

Isotropic   Anisotropic

© Infobase Publishing

An isotropic material has the same properties in all directions—for example, glass—whereas an anisotropic material has different properties depending on its orientation—for example, wood, which has a grain.

is traveling in the direction preferred by the orientation of the treated sunglass lens.

A PLM uses two polarizing filters (or polarizers, sometimes called polars for short), one called the polarizer (which seems obvious) and the analyzer (for reasons that will become obvious). The polarizer sits beneath the stage and has its preferred vibration direction set left-to-right (sometimes called the "east-west" direction, as on a map). The analyzer, aligned opposite that of the polarizer (that is, north-south), is located above the objectives; the analyzer can be manually slid into or out of the light path. If the analyzer is inserted with its orientation opposite that of the analyzer (at right angles), what should be seen? Nothing. The filters are said to be crossed, and no light can pass through the microscope to the viewer's eyes. The field of view appears black or very, very dark.

Information can be obtained both in plane-polarized light (only the polarizer in place) or with crossed polarizers (polarizer *and* analyzer in place). When transparent or translucent materials are viewed in plane-polarized light, they will appear much like they do when viewed in natural light until the specimen is rotated on the stage (on the optical axis of the microscope). As the item moves through the preferred orientation of the polarizer, changes may be seen in the brightness or color of the specimen. Try this with a dyed rayon fiber. This variation of color as the specimen moves through the orientation/direction of the light is called *pleochroism*. Only anisotropic materials display pleochroism because of the internal "grain" of the material. This causes the light to leave the material at varying angles, and when sunlight rays contact the oriented polarized filter, it is more or less blocked when it hits the polarizer.

Anisotropic materials split light into two component light rays. These two rays travel through the material at two different speeds. The internal organization of the material creates two "pathways" for the light rays, one fast and one slow. When an anisotropic material is placed under crossed polarizers and rotated on the microscope's optical axis, polarization colors result. These colors are caused by the interference of the two rays of light split by the anisotropic material interfering destructively with each other—that is, they cancel each other out to a

Normal light travels in all directions, whereas polarized light vibrates in only one direction. It is achieved by passing normal light through a special filter, called a polarizer. Sunglasses with polarized lenses reduce glare by blocking out light that reflects off glossy surfaces. *(Courtesy of the author)*

greater or lesser degree. The two light rays travel at different speeds (one faster than the other) through the specimen and therefore have different refractive indexes. *Birefringence* is the numerical difference between the refractive index of the fast light ray and the slow light ray. The faster light ray comes out of the sample before the slower light ray. Only the components of the two light rays traveling in the same direction in the same plane will recombine at the analyzer. Birefringence and other optical properties are very useful in polarized light microscopy to identify materials under the microscope. Textile fibers are a good example of this.

CEREAL MURDER IN SPOKANE

In February 1999, the home of James Cochran (all names have been changed) was engulfed in flames. After the fire was extinguished, Kevin, his 11-year-old son, was found to be missing. Kevin's backpack was located 15 miles (24.1 km) from his home, and two days later his body was found fully clothed at the bottom of a snowy embankment. The scene yielded a great deal of trace evidence, including gastric secretions (vomit), soil, metal turnings, building materials, paint, and soot. Although the evidence was circumstantial, it played a large role in the investigation of the homicide.

Investigators searched the home, the vehicles, areas around where Kevin and his items were found, and anywhere they believed James Cochran was on the day of the fire. A filing cabinet containing business documents was removed from the home, and it was determined that a large Rubbermaid garbage can was missing from Cochran's house. The clothing that Kevin was wearing exhibited a large amount of vomit. The boy's stomach contents, fingernail clippings, hand swabs, and clothing were collected as evidence. Cochran's pickup truck was searched for evidence; it contained traces of vomit in addition to clumps of crushed rock, soil, fresh grass, and pine needles. All of these things were potentially useful pieces of evidence to be examined.

The identification of vomit stains is based on the characterization of partially digested food ingredients and the presence of gastric enzymes. When a stain has been visually located, a stereobinocular microscope can be used to magnify the stain up to approximately 100 times. Individual particles within a stain can be particle-picked to a microscope slide for further analysis by polarized light microscopy. The stereobinocular microscope can be used to examine vomit stains in situ, showing the relationship of food particles as they were applied to the substrate (that is, the clothing). A PLM may be fitted with phase-contrast objectives and a specialized phase condenser lens. Phase contrast is a useful method to improve contrast when examining materials, such as food plant cells that have similar refractive indexes between grain boundaries. The PLM can magnify and resolve small particles down to the micrometer level, and it can determine many optical characteristics used in identification.

During an interview with Kevin's sisters, it was discovered that he was last seen eating cereal. Investigators therefore seized the three types of cereal from Cochran's home. Numerous slides of three cereals were prepared for examination and comparison by polarized light microscopy. The particles found in the vomit stains were similar to one type and dissimilar to the other types. The PLM, in conjunction with a few microchemical tests, revealed almost all of the known ingredients of the cereal. Microscopical examination showed similarities between the cereal, Kevin's vomit, and the stain in the bed of the pickup truck. The missing garbage can was also found, and it contained traces of the vomit that were microscopically consistent with the other stains.

Cochran was tied to the disappearance of his son and the transportation of the body to where it was found through trace analysis of the cereal bits in the vomit, metal particles, glitter particles, and paint samples. Investigators never got to present their case, however, as Cochran committed suicide in his jail cell. The value of the evidence would have been, without a doubt, powerful testimony at Cochran's trial.

Another case involving polarized light microscopy concerns a traffic accident. In September 1988, two friends, Jim and Tommy, were headed out for a night on the town. They were driving a Mercedes 560 SL convertible over the speed limit. The driver lost control of the car and struck a brick wall, ejecting both men. Witnesses only saw the men flying out of the vehicle; no one knew who was driving. After Tommy died due to the massive trauma of the accident, investigators were looking at a possible homicide, depending on who was the driver.

Trace evidence can be very important in such a case. The inside of the vehicle is essentially a closed space, and only Tommy and Jim occupied it. The officer did a complete accident reconstruction and investigation to determine the path of the vehicle and its occupants. Portions of the car's interior, windshield, airbags, carpets, and occupants' known hair samples were collected for examination. Although there were only a few physical items submitted to the laboratory originally, continued communication between the investigator and laboratory analyst allowed further submission of additional pieces of evidence.

The original submission included the windshield, some clothes from the car's occupants, shoes, break and accelerator pedals, and the left lower speaker grill. Head hair and eyebrow samples were also collected and submitted from the occupants. Using a stereomicroscope, it was determined that the lower stereo speaker grill and Jim's blue jeans had cross-transfer patterns, although the fibers on the speaker could have also come from Tommy's blue jeans. Almost all blue jeans are cotton-dyed with indigo dyes. Natural and synthetic indigo dyes are all chemically similar; therefore blue jeans typically have low evidentiary value.

Hair fragments and purple fibers were collected from the impact site on the driver's side of the windshield. No purple clothes had been submitted, so a request was placed with the investigator to get any remaining clothing from the occupants. No shoe-tread patterns were found on the brake pedals, but loose fibers were found and collected. The analyst then examined the shoes of both victims; Jim's shoes were found to have a large scuff, and they had caught some carpet-type fibers. The officer was contacted for a complete list of all evidence collected, with a specific request for any carpet or floor-mat samples collected from the wrecked car.

A second submission of evidence included shirts from both occupants and carpet samples from the various areas of the car and its floor mats. Jim's shirt turned out to be made of purple cotton, while Tommy's shirt was made of a denim material that had a crushed fiber area on the right sleeve. One carpet-type fiber found on Jim's shoe had the same microscopic characteristics and optical properties as those from a special Mercedes Benz floor mat that was only on the driver's side. Using infrared spectroscopy, it was determined that the scuffed material and the soles of Jim's shoes were composed of the same color and general polymer type as the designer floor mat.

Various microscopic characteristics of fibers may be identified by examinations using a PLM and a fluorescence microscope. The overall color, shape, and diameter of the fiber are noted. Any variation in color and whether the color is dyed or surface-dyed should be determined. Other important characteristics that may be observed using a PLM are a fiber's optical properties, such as its refractive index and birefringence. The cross-section of a fiber is also an important characteristic. Polarized light microscopy, fluorescence microscopy, and infrared spectroscopy were the only instruments used in this case.

A third submission of evidence was the passenger-side interior door panel, airbag, and steering wheel. The fabric impression on the passenger door panel was consistent with Jim's blue jeans, Tommy's blue jeans, and Tommy's denim shirt. Fibers collected from the airbag were examined using a stereomicroscope; they included blue cotton, white cotton, and purple cotton, which were consistent with Jim's clothing. The steering wheel was also examined with a stereomicroscope, and it had the same results as the airbag.

Jim was convicted of Tommy's murder after a long court proceeding. Although the defense's trace-evidence examiner had findings opposite those of the analysts, it was shown that improper comparisons of different magnifications were at fault. Also, original evidence had not been accounted for in the defense's findings. The trace evidence was invaluable evidence that proved Jim was driving.

OTHER MICROSCOPIC METHODS

Fluorescence is the luminescence of a substance excited by radiation. Luminescence can be subdivided into phosphorescence, which is characterized by long-lived emission (like the luminous numbers and hands on a "glow-in-the-dark" watch face) and fluorescence, in which the emission stops when the excitation stops (like a T-shirt glowing under a black light). The wavelength of the emitted fluorescence light is longer than that of the exciting radiation. In other words, a radiation of relatively high energy falls on a substance; the substance absorbs and/or converts (into heat, for example) a certain, small part of the energy, and most of the energy that is not absorbed by the substance is emitted again. Compared with the exciting radiation, the fluorescence radiation has lost energy, and its wavelength will be longer than that of the exciting radiation. Consequently, a fluorescing substance can be excited by near-ultraviolet-invisible radiation, and its fluorescent components are seen in the visible range.

In a fluorescence microscope, the specimen is illuminated with light of a short wavelength—for example, ultraviolet or blue. Part of this light is absorbed by the specimen and reemitted as fluorescence. To enable the comparatively weak fluorescence to be seen despite the strong illumination, the light used for excitation is filtered out by a secondary (barrier) filter placed between the specimen and the eye. This filter, in principle, should be fully opaque at the wavelength used for excitation and fully transparent at longer wavelengths so as to transmit the fluorescence. The fluorescent object is therefore seen as a bright image against a dark background.

It follows that a fluorescence microscope differs from a microscope used for conventional absorption microscopy, mainly in that it has a special light source and a pair of complementary filters. The lamp should be a powerful light source, rich in short wavelengths; high-pressure mercury arc lamps are the most common. A primary or excitation filter is placed somewhere between the lamp and the specimen. The filter, in combination with the lamp, should provide light over a comparatively narrow band of wavelengths corresponding to the absorption maximum of the fluorescent substance. The secondary barrier, or suppression, filter prevents the excitation light from reaching the observer's eye and is placed anywhere between the specimen and the eye.

5

Spectroscopy

Spectroscopy is the study of the interaction between matter and light energy. Spectroscopy is how forensic scientists characterize molecules and identify and compare items of evidence. The structure of atoms and molecules has been demonstrated by their interaction with light (electromagnetic radiation). The electromagnetic spectrum is divided into various regions. The different regions of the electromagnetic spectrum provide different information about the structure of molecules. Think of the spectrum as a series of waves flowing out of a source in all directions. Each wave has a specific length, noted in equations by the Greek letter lambda (λ), comprising the distance between two waves, measured at the same points on the waves.

Electromagnetic radiation can also be described in terms of its frequency (f), which is the number of waves that pass a given point in one second (also known as cycles per second, or hertz [Hz]). The relationship between wavelength and frequency is inverse (as frequency goes up, wavelength goes down and vice versa):

$$C = f/\lambda$$

where C is the speed of light.

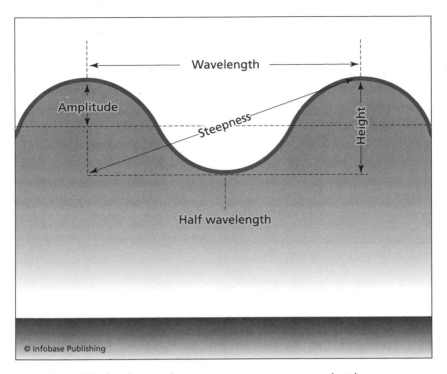

A wavelength is the distance between two waves, measured at the same points on the waves.

Another way to express frequency is by wave numbers. A wave number is the inverse of the wavelength measured in centimeters: A wave number is 1 cm⁻¹ (reciprocal centimeters). Interestingly, a wavelength can be expressed in any unit of length—millimeters, centimeters, or even meters. The units are chosen depending on which region of the electromagnetic spectrum is of interest in small, whole numbers. For example, in the ultraviolet region, nanometers (nm, 10^{-9} meters) are used to define the range, about 200–350 nm. A graph or plot of the energy response at each wavelength of light is called a spectrum (plural, spectra).

Physicists also describe light as tiny packets, or quanta (singular, quantum) of energy called photons. Energy is represented by the letter E in equations. The energy of a photon is related to wavelength (or, remembering their relationship, frequency) as shown in following equations:

$$E = hf$$
$$E = hc/\lambda$$

The *h* is Planck's constant, placed in the equation to ensure that the units are the same on both sides of the equation. Planck's constant changes as the units of energy, C, *h*, or λ change. Looking at the equations, it can be seen that as the frequency of light goes up, so does its energy, and as the wavelength goes up, the energy goes down.

At the far left of this electromagnetic spectrum are gamma rays. These are very energetic and can pass through matter; if they pass through living tissue, they can damage or destroy cells. Lower in energy are X-rays, which can pass through most matter but are deflected by dense matter, such as metal or bones. These materials appear opaque on an X-ray, while other, softer structures can be seen.

Lower in frequency and energy than X-rays is ultraviolet and visible radiation—two of the most important energy ranges for forensic science. The ultraviolet region is named that way because it is next to the violet area of the region of visible light (the light that human eyes can see as color). When light in this region encounters matter, only some of it passes through; the rest is absorbed, and this excites the electrons in the matter.

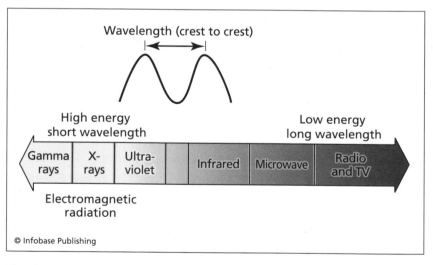

The electromagnetic spectrum is the range of all possible electromagnetic radiation. Many of the ranges of the spectrum are analytically useful in forensic science.

Below the red region of visible light is the infrared region (*infra* is Latin for "below"). When absorbed by matter, infrared radiation causes bonds between atoms in a molecule to vibrate like two weights on either end of a spring. The infrared region is also very important in the analysis of chemical evidence in forensic science.

Next is the microwave region, whose waves cause molecules to rotate or spin. This motion causes friction, which emits heat. This is how microwave ovens work: The microwaves are absorbed by water molecules in the food, and as they rotate, the heat cooks the food. At the lowest end of the spectrum are radio waves, which have large wavelengths and tiny frequencies.

INTERACTIONS OF MATTER AND LIGHT

How matter interacts with light of various frequencies is the basis of spectroscopy. These interactions can reveal information about the material under study. The interactions can even identify it to the exclusion of all other materials. The energy of the radiation elicits different changes in materials. Spectroscopists study the interactions of energy and matter (plotted on spectra) to identify materials and compare them, as noted in the following table.

RADIATION ENERGY INTERACTS WITH A MATERIAL TO DETERMINE MOLECULAR ENERGY CHANGE

Radiation Range	Molecular Energy Change
ultraviolet-visible	electronic, vibrational, and rotational
infrared	vibrational and rotational
far infrared/microwave	rotational
radio	nuclear spin flips

Different methods of spectroscopy yield different information about a molecule; used together, they can completely describe a molecule through its characteristic features. Mass spectrometry ionizes molecules by high-energy electrons. The mass-to-charge ratio of these ions is measured very accurately by electrostatic acceleration and magnetic field perturbation, providing a precise molecular weight. Ion fragmentation patterns may be related to the structure of the molecular ion. Ultraviolet-visible (or UV-Vis, for short, pronounced "yoo-vee-viz") spectroscopy excites molecules with relatively high-energy light. Some of this excitation is absorbed by the molecule's structure. A related type of spectroscopy, fluorescence spectroscopy, measures the long-wavelength light emitted by a substance when excited by a shorter-wavelength beam.

Infrared spectroscopy (IR) measures the absorption of lower-energy radiation. The IR beam causes vibrational and rotational excitation of groups of atoms within the molecule. Each functional group has a characteristic absorption pattern and is easily identified.

Raman spectroscopy is not widely employed in forensic science, but its importance is growing. When light is scattered by a molecule, most of the photons are elastically scattered—that is, they have the same energy (frequency) and, therefore, wavelength as the incoming photons. A small fraction gets scattered at frequencies different from, and usually lower than, the frequency of the incident light. The process leading to this is called the *Raman effect*. Raman scattering can occur with a change in the vibrational, rotational, or electronic energy of a molecule. A plot of intensity of scattered light versus energy difference is a Raman spectrum.

The two principal regions of light that are most important in characterizing evidence are the ultraviolet/visible (UV/vis) and the infra-red (IR) regions. All compounds absorb and reflect more or less light of certain wavelengths in the UV-Vis range—this is color. Humans see color only in the visible range of the electromagnetic spectrum; the eyes act like spectrometers, detecting colors that are transmitted through or reflected off an object. The light appears to be uniform but is actually composed of a range of wavelengths. The component colors of the visible portion can be separated by shining white light through a prism, which bends the light in according to wavelength. By convention, visible light is treated as a wave phenomenon and is described by wavelength or frequency.

The visible range covers approximately 400–800 nm of the spectrum. Red is the longest visible wavelength and violet the shortest. The order of the colors of the visible spectrum, in decreasing wavelength, can be

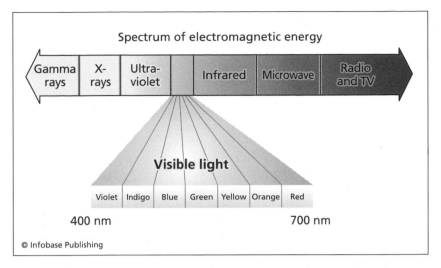

The visible range covers approximately 400–700 nm of the spectrum. The order of the colors of the visible spectrum, in decreasing wavelength, are red, orange, yellow, green, blue, indigo, and violet.

remembered by the "name" Roy G. Biv: red, orange, yellow, green, blue, indigo, and violet.

MATTER IS WHAT MATTERS

All matter consists of negatively charged electrons that inhabit regions called orbitals, which exist in approximately concentric spheres around the nucleus of each atom. The nucleus is made up of positively charged protons and neutral neutrons. In a neutral atom, there are equal numbers of electrons (-) and protons (+), so there is no net positive or negative charge. When atoms combine to make molecules (the building bricks of compounds and materials), they do so by sharing or donating/accepting electrons to form covalent (sharing) or ionic (donating/accepting) bonds. The electrons that are shared are in the outermost orbital, called the outer shell. Electrons in the outer shell can be promoted to a higher energy level (closer to the nucleus) by absorbing energy from the outside. The atom or molecule can only absorb the exact amount (quantum) of energy that corresponds to the difference in energy between the occupied and unoccupied energy levels. Therefore, a molecule will absorb energy and promote an electron only if it encounters a photon of the proper energy. One can visualize these energy levels to be like rungs on a ladder: It can be on one rung or the next, but it cannot be between the rungs.

When a substance is exposed to UV/visible radiation, it will absorb photons of specific wavelengths (and therefore particular frequencies). Remember, some of the radiation is absorbed and some reflected; the portion reflected in the visible range is what is called color. If the sample compound does not absorb light of a given wavelength, then the intensity coming into the sample is equal to the intensity coming out, or:

$$I = I_o$$

However, if the sample compound absorbs light, then I is less than I_0, and this intensity difference may be plotted on a graph versus wavelength (a spectrum). The intensity difference may be displayed as the amount transmitted (transmittance or T), where $T = I/I_0$, or the amount absorbed (absorbance, or A), where $A = \log I_0/I$. Logically, if no absorption has occurred, T = 1.0 and A = 0. Most spectrometers display absorbance on the vertical axis, and the commonly observed range is from 0 (100 percent transmittance) to 2 (1 percent transmittance). The wavelength of maximum absorbance is a characteristic value, designated as λ_{max}, pronounced "lambda max." Different compounds may have very different absorption maxima (singular, maximum) and absorbances.

The peaks in a UV/visible spectrum tend to be few in number and broad in shape. This reflects the way UV/visible radiation is absorbed: Only a few electrons can be promoted in an average molecule. Few wavelengths exist where a workable number of photons will be absorbed. It is the vagueness of these peaks that limits their usefulness, and they are not commonly used for absolute identification of chemical substances. The typical UV/visible range spectrum is not sufficiently unique to identify a substance from all other similar substances. Because of the wide variety of colors and chemicals to produce those colors, UV/visible spectra are useful in comparing colored substances, like fibers, that become evidence.

WHAT MAKES COLOR?

Not every substance absorbs energy in the UV/visible range. Those molecules that do have "submolecules," or groups called chromophores. The chromophores will absorb UV/visible radiation in certain wavelengths but not in others. For example, if a substance absorbs most energies except those in the red range, the substance will appear red. When the spectrum is plotted in absorbance, it will have high peaks except for the red range; the converse is true if it is plotted in transmittance. Some chromophores will absorb strongly or weakly, depending on their size and structure (number of electrons that they can share, donate, or accept). The magnitude of λ reflects both the size of the chromophore and the probability that light of a given wavelength will be absorbed when it strikes the chromophore.

A UV/visible spectrum is collected by a spectrophotometer, an instrument that is designed to detect and analyze radiation in the UV/visible range; spectrometers for other electromagnetic ranges are also available. The way this instrument works is pretty straightforward. A beam of light from a source (a bulb that emits radiation in specific ranges, in this case, UV/visible) is separated into its individual component wavelengths by a prism or diffraction grating (a filter that breaks light up much like a prism). Each single wavelength (or monochromatic) beam in turn is split into two equal-intensity beams of the same wavelength. One beam, the sample beam, passes through the sample being analyzed. The other beam, the reference beam, passes through the system without hitting the sample. The intensities of these light beams are then measured by electronic detectors and compared. The intensity of the reference beam, which should have suffered little or no light absorption, is defined as I_0. The intensity of the sample beam is defined as I. All this happens in a matter of seconds, thanks to the advanced computers and software now available for scientific equipment.

MICROSPECTROPHOTOMETRY

Suppose a forensic scientist receives individual colored fibers as evidence and wants to collect visible spectra to compare their colors and their infrared spectra to identify them chemically. None of the sampling methods discussed so far for either technique are designed to accept a single, thin fiber. To analyze these types of samples, a microscope can be joined with a spectrophotometer to make a microspectrophotometer. A microspectrophotometer can be thought of as a microscope, a light source, a monochromator, and a detector. The object (a fiber in this case) is mounted on the stage of the microscope, and all of the light is focused on the object. The detector detects the light transmitted by the object. There are microspectrophotometers for visible and UV light and for the infrared region. Because much of what forensic scientists receive as evidence may be microscopic, microspectrophotometers are invaluable tools in the modern forensic laboratory.

Case Review: The Importance of Color

On the morning of May 8, 1985, the victim left his house to attend classes at a local college. After finding her son's car locked near her house, the victim's mother contacted authorities. Two days later, she received a call with instructions to pick up a package in a local phone booth, which would explain what had happened to her son. When she picked up the package, it contained a ransom note demanding $200,000 in exchange for her son. Three days later she received a call with instructions to leave the money by a statue in a park. The money was left along with a radio-tracking device concealed under a false bottom in a briefcase, courtesy of the authorities. An individual in a 1975 blue Oldsmobile picked it up and was arrested later that day.

The victim was found on May 28 in an old icehouse. He had been shot three times and had head wounds inflicted by a square-edged instrument. Evidence submitted to the FBI laboratory included the following items: hair samples from the suspect, hair samples from the victim, a sample from a throw rug from the Oldsmobile trunk, a trunk-liner sample from the 1975 blue Oldsmobile, the victim's clothing (blue jeans and shirt), hairs from various locations (trunk and door frame used to cover the body), fibers and a thread from the door covering the victim, purple gloves from the suspect's Camaro, vacuum particles from the Oldsmobile's trunk, debris from the Oldsmobile trunk liner, and hair and fibers from the Oldsmobile trunk liner.

The criteria used to make a determination that a fiber or animal hair is consistent with having originated from a particular source involve the comparison and matching of numerous microscopic characteristics

INFRARED SPECTROPHOTOMETRY

Infrared spectrophotometry is one type of vibrational spectroscopy, a spectroscopic technique where molecular vibrations are analyzed. To get a better handle on infrared spectrophotometry, the principles of simple harmonic motion must be discussed. Imagine two balls connected with

and/or numerous optical properties, which hairs and fibers exhibit. In this case, a match was reported between hairs recovered from the trunk and the known sample from the victim. Black rayon fibers found on the victim's clothing were matched to fibers in the composition of what was left of a trunk liner from the Oldsmobile. Also, matching yellow acrylic, maroon polypropylene, and some animal hairs were recovered from both the trunk and the victim's clothing. Testimony at the trial regarding hair and fiber evidence stated in part that "it is the basis of an extremely strong association between the trunk of the car and the victim, and in my opinion, the probability or chance that the victim was not in the trunk in this case is extremely small." Although the hair and fiber evidence was only part of the case, it was useful in establishing relationships between the trunk of the Oldsmobile and the victim.

The diversity of colors in textiles is astounding. The dyeing process is chemically complicated with many manufacturing variations. Based on the desired end-product effects—the fiber substrate and the type of dye used—there are more than 12 different application categories for textile dyes. Very few textiles are colored with only one dye, and even a simple dye may be put through eight to 10 processing steps to achieve a final dye form, shade, and strength. More than 7,000 dyes are used worldwide. When all of these factors are considered, it becomes apparent that it is virtually impossible to dye textiles in a continuous method—that is, dyeing separate batches of fibers or textiles is the rule rather than the exception. This color variability has the potential to be very significant in forensic fiber comparisons.

a spring. A ball will oscillate (vibrate back and forth on the spring) at a certain frequency, depending on the masses of the balls and how stiff the spring is. This is a simple harmonic oscillator. For example, a ball with a low mass is lighter and moves more easily than one with a high mass. The following rules determine this oscillation frequency:

- Lower masses oscillate at a higher frequency than higher masses.

- Very stiff springs are deformed with more difficulty and return to their original shape quickly.

- Weak springs are easily deformed and take longer to return to their original shape.

- Therefore, stiffer springs oscillate at higher frequencies than weak ones.

The balls and springs are analogous to a chemical bond between two atoms. The atomic bonds can be thought of as simple harmonic oscillators, where the bond is the spring and the two atoms (or groups of atoms) are the balls. Every atom has a different mass. The various bonds—single, double, and triple—all have different stiffness. So each type of molecule, a combination of atoms and bonds, has its own particular harmonic frequency.

Imagine a violin. If the E string were plucked, it would vibrate at that frequency and make the E note. If another string were plucked, the E string might also vibrate because some of energy from the vibrating string was transferred to the E string, causing it to vibrate as well. This analogy also works with molecules. When a molecule vibrates at a certain frequency and encounters another vibration of *exactly* the same frequency, the oscillator will absorb that energy.

All the simple harmonic oscillators in molecules vibrate all the time. Infrared (IR) light vibrates in the same frequency range as vibrating molecules. On the immediate high-energy side of the visible spectrum lies the ultraviolet, and on the low-energy side is the infrared. The portion of the infrared region most useful for analysis of organic compounds is not immediately adjacent to the visible spectrum but has a wavelength range from 2,500 to 16,000 nm, with a corresponding frequency range from $1.9*10^{13}$ to $1.2*10^{14}$ Hz. If a vibrating molecule (or just a molecule, because they all vibrate) encounters infrared light, those frequencies in the infrared light exactly matching the frequencies of the harmonic oscillators in the molecule will be absorbed. Because they have absorbed the energy of the infrared light, their amplitude will increase—the springs stretch further. Whatever light was not absorbed by the molecule is transmitted through the sample.

Traditional IR instruments took quite a long time to scan every frequency in the IR portion of the spectrum. The instrument had to measure the absorption at frequency 1 (and measure it multiple times to reduce error) and then "move" to frequency 2, and so on. With the advent of the Fourier transform algorithm, infrared spectroscopy became faster, more reliable, and a mainstay in chemistry laboratories around the world.

Any signal can be described in either time or frequency. The transformation can get a little complicated. The input signal must be separated into many simpler signals, and then the system or instrument must be trained how to respond to the incoming signal. This is accomplished by an algorithm called the Fourier transform. Data is dealt with in the time domain most frequently, such as the heart-rate tracking on a piece of hospital equipment or an oscilloscope at the local automobile mechanic's shop. The vertical dimension is the signal's amplitude, whereas the horizontal dimension is time. The frequency domain is like the heart beats per minute being lined up along an axis with the number of beats stacked up like a bar graph.

The Fourier transform was developed by Baron Jean-Baptiste-Joseph Fourier around 1810 while researching the conduction of heat. It is important because it can relate numerous physical variables, such as time and frequency. Fourier transform spectroscopy (FTS) became practical in the early 1950s when research groups assembled and tested high-resolution spectrometers, demonstrating that certain theoretical advantages could be achieved. During the 1950s and 1960s, despite advances in the laboratory, the development of FTS was limited by the high cost and computational power of computers. In 1965, James Cooley and John Tukey developed a fast Fourier transform (FFT) algorithm that allowed Fourier transforms to be run efficiently on computers. The FFT reduced the computation time by several orders of magnitude and made transforming large spectra feasible. As often happens in science, it turned out that Cooley and Tukey had independently "reinvented" the FFT, based on an algorithm developed by Carl Frederich Gauss in 1805.

The FFT algorithm appears as follows:

$$F(v) = \int_{-\infty}^{\infty} f(t)e^{-i(2\pi)vt} dt$$

and

$$f(t) = \int_{-\infty}^{\infty} 2\pi F(v) e^{i(2\pi)vt} dt$$

Today commercial Fourier transform spectrometers are the norm in many applications. Many spectroscopic techniques have benefited by the application of the FTS, such as Fourier transform-Raman spectroscopy (FT-Raman), Fourier transform microwave (FTMW) spectroscopy and Fourier transform NMR spectroscopy.

In addition to the facile rotation of groups about single bonds, molecules experience a wide variety of vibrational motions, characteristic of their component atoms. Consequently, all organic compounds will absorb infrared radiation that corresponds in energy to these vibrations. Infrared spectrometers, similar in principle to the UV-visible spectrometer, permit chemists to obtain absorption spectra of compounds that are a reflection of their molecular structure. Each different chemical bond in the molecule has its own characteristic vibrations, and each bond can undergo a number of different kinds of vibrations.

However, unlike UV-visible absorptions, there are *many* infrared absorptions in each type of molecule. Remembering the example of the E string on the violin, imagine closing your eyes while someone else strums a stringed instrument. A violin sounds different from a harp. These multiple vibrations create a pattern of response that allows for the identification of the grouped vibrations. Even the slightest change in the composition of a molecule will result in a different infrared spectrum. Thus, the infrared spectrum of a pure substance will be unique and can be used to unequivocally identify that substance. Infrared spectrophotometry is one of the two analytical techniques, along with gas chromatography-mass spectrometry, that can be used for identification of substances such as drugs.

6

Chromatography

Chromatography is the process of separating small amounts of substances from a mixture by the rate at which they move through or along medium (the stationary phase). Most methods of chromatography involve dissolving the mixture in a solvent (the eluent), though it is vaporized in gas chromatography. Substances move at different rates because they vary in their solubility and their attraction to the medium.

Column chromatography involves the use of components in a mixture that are separated in a column containing a solvent and a material that attracts molecules. Gas chromatography involves a vaporized mixture that is separated as it passes along a heated column in a stream of inert gas. The amount of compound in each phase depends on its relative affinity for the two phases. The proportion to which a compound distributes itself between two phases, which is termed the *partition coefficient,* is different for different compounds.

In 1903, the Russian botanist M. S. Tswett devised a separation method called liquid column chromatography. Tswett separated structurally similar yellow and green chloroplast pigments obtained

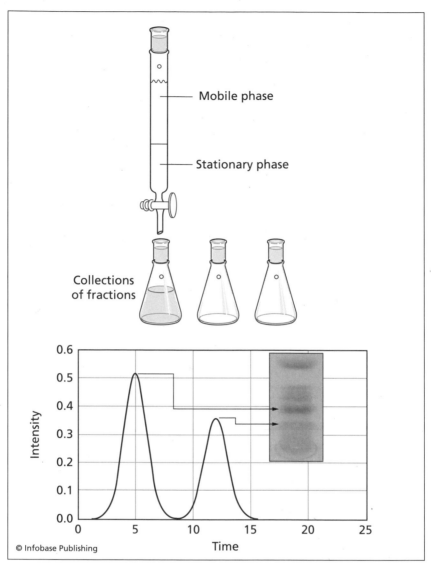

Mobile phase

Stationary phase

Collections of fractions

© Infobase Publishing

Chromatography is the family of techniques for the separation of mixtures. It involves passing a substance dissolved in a mobile phase through a stationary phase, which separates the analyte (the material of interest) from other molecules in the substance. Compounds with a greater affinity for the stationary phase lag behind those with less affinity and appear later in a chromatogram (bottom, first peak), whereas the compounds also can be separated visually (see silica plate, left). The graphic is arranged for instructional purposes. (Courtesy of the author) from leaf extracts by placing an extract into the top of a column of calcium carbonate particles and then washing the column with carbon disulfide (by gravity flow of the solvent). The colored pigments formed visible bands that separated as they moved down the column. Thus, Tswett coined the term *chromatography* from the Greek meaning "color writing," although he realized the method was applicable to colorless compounds.

Modern liquid column chromatography, now called high performance liquid chromatography (HPLC) or just liquid chromatography (LC), was made possible by technical advances in equipment, columns, and column-packing materials. It enables the user to perform rapid, efficient separation of complex mixtures of organic, inorganic, pharmaceutical, and biochemical compounds.

The objective is to move different materials through a column at different velocities so that they exit the column at different times. The molecules of substance 1 and 2 are also swept along at the velocity of the mobile phase, and they would all exit the column at the same time were it not for the stationary phase. It is the time each molecule spends in the stationary phase that determines when it will exit the column. Substance 1 (first peak) spends less time in the stationary phase and therefore has a shorter retention time than substance 2 (second peak).

The separation of individual components is of prime importance in chromatography. The degree of separation depends on the difference in retention times and the sharpness of the peaks in question. Resolution is a measure of the degree of separation.

GAS CHROMATOGRAPHY

Gas chromatography (GC) uses an inert gas mobile phase (such as helium or nitrogen) and typically a high-molecular-weight silicone coating on the walls of the column (a coated column) or a coated packing in the column (a packed column). GCs can be outfitted with a variety of detectors. Flame ionization detectors ionize the compounds in a flame and measure the number of ions generated. Thermal conductivity detectors measure heat-conducting or specific heat-altered properties in the substance. Electron capture detectors use changes in the detector's standardized electrical charge caused by samples with high electron affinity to create the signal.

Two types of columns are generally used: packed and capillary. Packed columns contain a fine, inert, solid support material coated with the stationary phase. Most packed columns are 5–30 feet (1.5–10 m) in length and have an internal diameter of 2–4 mm. Capillary columns, sometimes known as open tubular columns, have an internal diameter of a few tenths of a millimeter. Capillary columns fall into three categories: wall-coated open tubular, support-coated open tubular, and fused silica open tubular. Wall-coated columns are capillary tubes with stationary phase-coated walls; support-coated columns have their inner walls lined with a support material (usually diatomaceous earth) that is coated with the stationary phase. Both types of capillary column are more efficient than packed columns. Fused silica open tubular columns have much thinner walls than glass capillary columns and are stronger because of the silica coating. These columns are flexible and can be wound into coils. They have the advantages of physical strength, flexibility, and low reactivity.

GAS CHROMATOGRAPHY/MASS SPECTROMETRY

Gas chromatography/mass spectrometry (GC/MS) couples a gas chromatograph with a mass spectrometer, capitalizing on the chromatograph's separation capabilities and the spectrometer's power at identifying a substance's molecular structure. A high-voltage electron beam (70 eV or more) is used to shatter molecules that pass through it, creating fragment ions. The ions are sorted in the analyzer by mass and then detected. The mass spectroscopist recognizes masses of fragments and deduces the structure of the unknown substance from the fragment ions; libraries of known substances and their fragmentation patterns are available.

LIQUID CHROMATOGRAPHY (LC)

Solvent proportioning valves deliver precisely controlled volumes of solvent from the reservoirs to the mixing chamber. High-pressure pumping systems transfer the solvent mixture from the mixing chamber to the injector valve and are usually capable of outputs up to 5,000 psi and reproducible flow deliveries of 0.1–10 mL/min. High-performance columns that provide minimum broadening of separating sample bands are the heart of the liquid chromatograph. Columns are made from 3–25 cm lengths of stainless steel tubing with inner diameters of 1–20 mm. Columns are packed with small (3–50 μm) particles that constitute the stationary phase. The choice of a stationary phase/mobile phase combination is determined by the nature of the separation problem.

In ion-exchange chromatography, the stationary bed has an ionically charged surface of opposite charge to the sample ions. This technique is used almost exclusively with ionic or ionizable samples. The stronger the charge on the sample, the more strongly it will be attracted to the ionic surface, and thus the longer it will take to elute. The mobile phase is an aqueous buffer, where both pH and ionic strength are used to control elution time.

Size-exclusion chromatography, also known as gel-permeation chromatography, separates sample molecules on the basis of their physical size. The stationary phase is a gel with pores of a particular average size. Molecules that are too large to permeate the pores move directly through the column and appear first in the chromatogram. Small molecules permeate the pores, follow a long path through the pore matrix, and have longer retention times. The mobile phase is chosen for its ability to dissolve the sample and move through the matrix (low viscosity).

7

Forensic DNA

DNA typing is an example of a revolutionary technology in the forensic and natural sciences. Advances in DNA analysis have not only allowed for personal identification from biological material but has greatly increased the kinds of biological material that can be analyzed. In the mid-1980s, Sir Alec Jeffreys developed the first effective method for isolating and comparing human DNA for forensic applications. This science has advanced to the point where forensic scientists are able to compare specific parts of the human genetic code.

DNA (deoxyribonucleic acid) is a molecule that is found in nearly all living cells; the only relevant exceptions are red blood cells and nerve cells. DNA is a special polymer, a molecule made up of repeating simpler units called monomers. Two types of DNA have forensic value: genomic (also called nuclear) and mitochondrial.

GENOMIC DNA

A genomic DNA molecule can be thought of as a pair of ladders twisted around each other. The poles of the ladder are identical in all living things. They are made up of alternating sugar molecules (deoxyribose) and phosphates. Hanging off of each sugar molecule is one of four bases (nucleotides): adenine (A), guanine (G), cytosine (C), and thymine (T). When an adenine base and a thymine base come into proximity, they form a bond to each other. Likewise, when cytosine and guanine get near each other, they will bond. Thymine can only bond with adenine (and vice versa), while guanine can only bond with cytosine (and vice versa). The DNA molecule consists of the sugar-phosphate backbones connected by linked pairs of bases that can only be A-T, T-A, G-C, or C-G. The order in which the base pairs occur *along* the ladder is not governed by similar rules; the pairs can occur in any order. The order of the base pairs constitutes a language of sorts—a genetic code—for translating DNA into the characteristics of an organism. Think of it this way: Everyone has a 10-digit phone number (three-digit area code, three-digit exchange, and a four-digit number), but the digits must be dialed in the correct sequence to get to a particular person.

Most cells in the human body have a nucleus (not to be confused with the atomic nucleus) where most of the cell's functions are controlled. In humans, the DNA in the nucleus is arranged into 46 structures called chromosomes. The chromosomes are arranged in 23 pairs; one member of each pair of chromosomes comes from the father and the other member comes from the mother. Male sperm contain 23 chromosomes, and the female ovum (egg) also contains 23. When sperm and egg unite, the 23 chromosomes from the sperm and the egg pair up, forming the 46 found in every nucleated cell in the offspring. One pair of chromosomes determines the sex of the individual. For females, both chromosomes are of the "X" type. In males, one of the chromosomes is X and the other is Y.

Within the long strands of DNA are sections called genes. The base pair sequences in genes code for specific things; think of the base pairs as letters and the genes as words. The ordering of the base pairs in genes provides the chemical instructions to manufacture particular proteins in the body. These genetic instructions are coded on RNA (ribonucleic acid). Each gene codes for a particular characteristic protein. Surprisingly (or maybe not), more than 99 percent of all human DNA is exactly the same: It codes for the things that make us all human. The rest of the

DNA (less than 1 percent) contains the genetic information that differentiates one human being from another.

Genes that determine a person's individual characteristics are found in particular locations on the chromosomes. Some traits are determined

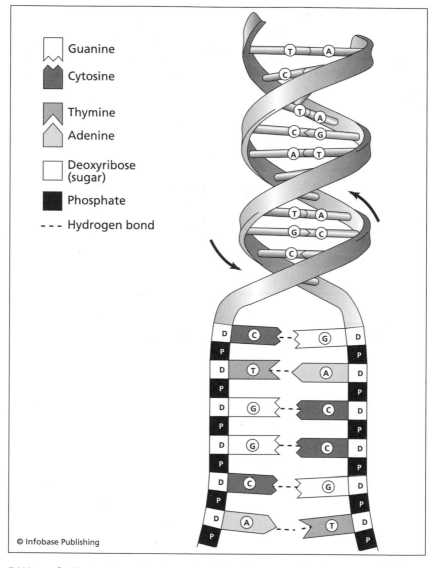

© Infobase Publishing

DNA is a fairly simple molecule made of four bases attached to a sugar and phosphate backbone.

by a single gene on one chromosome. Others, such as eye color, are determined by multiple genes on several chromosomes. Simple observation of peoples' eyes indicates that there must be considerable variation in this gene, since some people have brown eyes, others blue or green, and many have eye colors that are somewhere in between colors. For example, a person may inherit the eye-color gene that codes for blue eyes from her mother and the same gene that codes for brown eyes from her father. The actual eye color that the child has is determined by genetic rules that may be somewhat complicated. The two different eye color genes are variants of the same gene (eye color); these variant types of genes are called alleles. If a person inherits the same form of a gene from the mother and the father, that person is said to be homozygous with respect to that gene.

Some characteristics may exist in many forms or alleles. Each person will inherit one allele from the mother and one from the father. If there are a large number of such alleles, then there would be much variation among human beings at this location (or locus, Latin for "place"). This provides the basis for some kinds of DNA typing wherein the variation of alleles at several loci are exploited to subdivide a population into many subgroups. There may be so many of these subgroups that virtual individuality can be achieved.

A person's genetic makeup is his genotype, the genetic description of his alleles. A person's genotype as expressed in a particular environment is called the phenotype. For example, your genotype may code for brown hair. Living in a city with little sunshine and with clouds most of the time, a person with brown hair color would be expressing it (phenotype) pretty much the way it was coded for genetically. But if that person, moves to a sunny, warm climate and gets a job working outdoors, the sun would bleach his hair out, and his phenotype would change; however, his genotype would not.

There are two types of variability in alleles. The first type is sequence polymorphisms (*poly* means "many" and *morph* means "shape"). An example of a sequence polymorphism in DNA would be:

1. CTCG<u>A</u>TTAAGG   CTCG<u>G</u>TTAAGG

2. GAGC<u>T</u>AATTCC   GAGC<u>C</u>AATTCC

The two sequences of double-stranded DNA are exactly the same except at the location indicated by the underlined letters.

The other type of variation in DNA is called length polymorphism. Consider the following variation in a part of the song "Happy Birthday":

Happy birthday to you
Happy birthday to to you
Happy birthday to to to you
Happy birthday to to to to you

These phrases are all the same except for the "to," which repeats a different number of times in each line. Now consider the length polymorphism that occurs in the following DNA sequences:

C A T G T A C - C A T G T A C
G T A C A T G - G T A C A T G

C A T G T A C - C A T G T A C - C A T G T A C - C A T G T A C
G T A C A T G - G T A C A T G - G T A C A T G - G T A C A T G

Both of these consist of a seven-base-pair sequence that is repeated. In the first case it is repeated twice; in the second example it is repeated four times. Because the repeats are next to each other, without any base pairs in between, these are referred to as tandem repeats (like a tandem bicycle). If these are found at the same locus in different people or in the same person, then this locus is described as having a variable number of tandem repeats.

POPULATION GENETICS

In DNA analysis, locations, or loci, on the gene that are polymorphic (more than one shape) are purposely chosen. These loci exhibit variation among members of a population, and the more variation that occurs at a locus, the more specific the result will be. For example, in the ABO blood system, type A blood is present in about 42 percent of the Caucasian population, type O is present in about 43 percent, type B about 10 percent, and type AB in about 5 percent. Although variation exists, it is not very discriminating: Even the rarest form eliminates only 95 percent of the Caucasian population. That may sound like it could be useful, but in a population of 10 million people, there would still be half a million people with the same blood type!

Forensic DNA analysis uses multiple loci, and where several alleles exist at a particular locus, the frequency of occurrence can be determined for each allele. The frequency of occurrence of *all* of these alleles can be determined by multiplying their individual frequencies of occurrence. As an example, toss a coin: The frequency of occurrence for heads is 0.5 (50 percent) because there are only two equally probable outcomes, heads and tails. Now toss two coins: the frequency of occurrence for *two* heads (both coins coming up heads) is 0.25 (25 percent). There are four possible outcomes from tossing a coin twice:

Coin 1	Coin 2
heads	heads
heads	tails
tails	heads
tails	tails

Only one of these four outcomes is two heads, 1 in 4 or 25 percent. Another way to think of this is $0.5 \times 0.5 = 0.25$. The frequency of occurrence for three heads from three coins is 0.125, and so on.

The multiplication rule works only if the probability of each event is independent of the other events. In genetics, the occurrence of each allele must be independent of all of the other alleles being measured. A large number of loci contain alleles that exhibit such independence. The multiplication rule can yield gene types that are so rare that the chances of finding more than one person at random within a population with the same genetic makeup are essentially zero.

FORENSIC DNA TYPING

In 1984, a major breakthrough in forensic science took place at the University of Leicester in England. Dr. Alec Jeffreys was studying a substance called myoglobin and the phenomenon that parts of the gene did not seem to have a role in the production of myoglobin. These parts were made up of repeating base sequences of approximately the same length. Jeffreys found the number of repeats differed from person to person and variation was high; therefore he dubbed these regions as *hypervariable*. It occurred to Jeffreys that this variation could be forensically useful as a way of identifying people. He then replicated the sequences and extracted the DNA. One of Jeffreys's discoveries was that humans had multiple hypervariable regions. The technique he developed of isolating and analyzing these regions became known as "DNA fingerprinting" and was the basis for modern forensic DNA typing.

DNA recovered from crime scenes (blood, semen, or other body fluids) is often found in minute quantities or is very badly degraded. This makes it difficult if not impossible to analyze the DNA; as the DNA degrades, it breaks down into smaller and smaller chunks. The original DNA methods required long strands of intact DNA. A method was developed that provided for the replication of DNA into millions of copies. The method, called polymerase chain reaction (PCR), produced sufficient DNA for analysis. The PCR process amplifies preselected segments of DNA millions of times using enzymes, much in the same way a photocopier can make many copies of a document.

The most powerful current method for DNA analysis is called STR analysis, for short tandem repeats. STRs are sequences of short strands of DNA that repeat in tandem. In the current methodology, STRs from 13 different loci are analyzed. The DNA is first amplified at these loci by PCR. The amplified DNA consists almost entirely of the repeats. The STRs are chemically labeled with a fluorescent dye. The DNA is then run through an instrument that uses a laser to excite the dye. The fluorescing dyes are detected by the instrument, and it converts the results into a series of peaks, like a chromatogram. An enormous amount of data is generated during the analysis because all 13 loci are run at the same time.

The population frequency ranges for each allele at each locus are known. Using the rule of multiplication, the population frequencies for all of the alleles can be calculated. The probability of having a DNA type from all of the 13 loci is extremely small—about one in several billion or even trillion. Given that the U.S. population is about 300 million people, the chance of any two people at random having the same exact DNA at all 13 loci is extremely remote. The frequency of a 13-STR profile is one in 3.8 *quadrillion*. Quadrillion is what comes after trillion (which is what comes after billion). One quadrillion is a "1" followed by 15 zeros, or

1,000,000,000,000,000

To put this into perspective, compared with the world population, 3.8 quadrillion is

3,800,000,000,000,000
6,000,000,000,000

This number is accepted by some forensic laboratories as being sufficiently large that it constitutes individualization. Other laboratories do not accept this and report out the statistics as numbers—just very large numbers.

MITOCHONDRIAL DNA (mtDNA)

Not all human DNA is located in the cell's nucleus. Just as bodies have organs, so do cells; they are called organelles ("little organs"), and they exist in the cell but outside the nucleus. Some organelles have their own packets of DNA; one of these packets is the mitochondria (singular, mitochondrion). Mitochondria function for cells much like our lungs do for us: They help us remove processed gasses and remove waste. The proteins that control these functions are manufactured according to a genetic code separate from that in the nucleus that is housed within the mitochondria.

The following is a list of the differences between mitochondrial DNA (or mtDNA) and genomic DNA:

- mtDNA is circular in shape, unlike the twisted double ladder of genomic DNA.

- mtDNA is shorter/smaller than genomic DNA, but thousands of copies of mtDNA exist in each mitochondrion, compared with only a few copies of genomic DNA in a human cell.

- mtDNA contains a noncoding region of 1,100 base pairs. This region does not code for any particular proteins; it just acts as a "spacer" for the sequence. Within this noncoding region, there are two areas that are extremely variable in their sequences (so-called hypervariable regions). During a cell's reproduction of DNA, certain base pairs will not be replicated exactly; because they do not code for anything, it is sort of "no harm, no foul." But this means that many differences will exist between mtDNA from two people with different mothers (see next bullet).

- All mtDNA comes from the mother; no mtDNA comes from a father. Every descendant of a woman should have the same mtDNA, barring mutations. This makes mtDNA very powerful for tracing family generations through the maternal side of the family.

- mtDNA often shows a high degree of variation between unrelated people, making it a powerful tool in forensic typing. Some sequences appear the same between nonmaternally related people, but this is a very small percentage of the population.

Mitochondrial DNA may be the last, best hope to identify people. A very hardy molecule, mtDNA survives in numerous quantities in hairs, bone, and teeth. Often, these are the only remains of individuals who are badly decomposed or are victims of mass disasters, such as plane crashes or bombings. Not all forensic science laboratories that perform genomic DNA analysis also do mtDNA analysis. Those that do generally use DNA sequencing; they determine the entire base pair sequence in the two hypervariable regions of the mtDNA, rather than relying on length polymorphism.

The advent of forensic mtDNA in the mid-1990s heralded a new era of biological analysis in law enforcement. This was especially true for hairs, as it offered a way to add information to microscopic hair examinations. The microscopic comparison of human hairs has been accepted scientifically and legally for decades. Mitochondrial DNA sequencing added another test for assessing the significance of attributing a hair to an individual. Neither the microscopic nor molecular analysis alone, or together, provides positive identification. The two methods complement each other in the information they provide. For example, mtDNA typing can often distinguish between hairs from different sources although they have similar, or insufficient, microscopic hair characteristics. Hair comparisons with a microscope, however, can often distinguish between samples from maternally related individuals, while mtDNA analysis is "blind."

In a recent study, the results of microscopic and mitochondrial examinations of human hairs submitted to the FBI Laboratory for analysis

The First Forensic Use of mtDNA

Mitochondrial DNA (mtDNA) evidence was introduced for the first time in a Tennessee murder prosecution against 27-year-old Paul Ware in September 1996. Ware was accused of the rape and murder of Lindsey Green, a four-year-old girl. The defendant claimed that another man in the home, a babysitter, had made it look as if Ware had committed the crime. Ware was found drunk and asleep next to the child's body. The victim's blood was not found on the suspect; the suspect's semen was not found on her. However, during the autopsy, a small red hair was discovered in the throat of the victim, and several small red hairs had been found in a bed at the crime scene.

Mitochondrial DNA was extracted from two of the hairs recovered from the crime scene—one from the throat of the victim and one from the bedsheet in the room where the rape was alleged to have occurred. Mitochondrial DNA was also extracted from a sample of Paul Ware's saliva and from the victim's blood. The mtDNA sequence from the hair in the throat and from the hair found on the sheet were compared and found to be exact mtDNA matches of each other. They were further compared to the saliva sample of the defendant and found to match. Each of these three mtDNA samples was compared to the known mtDNA sequence of the victim, and they did not match. Ware was convicted of murder and sentenced to life imprisonment.

Mitochondrial DNA is now routinely used in cases of criminal investigation, personal identity, and disaster victim identification.

were reviewed. Of 170 hair examinations, there were 80 microscopic associations; importantly, only nine were excluded by mtDNA. Also, 66 hairs that were considered either unsuitable for microscopic examinations or yielded inconclusive microscopic associations were able to be analyzed with mtDNA. Only six of these hairs did not provide enough mtDNA, and another three yielded inconclusive results. This study demonstrates the strength of combining the two techniques.

It is important to understand that microscopy is not a "screening test" and mtDNA analysis is not a "confirmatory test." Either method can provide important information to an investigation. One test is not better than the other because they both analyze different characteristics. The only question left, then, is the following one posed by James Robertson of the Australian Federal Police:

> To what extent preliminary microscopic examinations should be conducted prior to DNA analysis . . . it may well be the case that there will *be little if any reduction in the level of microscopic examination as it will be both necessary and desirable to eliminate as many questioned hairs as possible* and concentrate mtDNA analysis on only key hairs. [emphasis added]

The data in the FBI study support the usefulness of both methods—and this is echoed in the expanding use of both microscopical and mitochondrial DNA examinations of hairs in forensic cases. An example of this usefulness is a case from Florida involving the abduction, sexual assault, and murder of a nine-year-old girl. Among the numerous evidence types encountered in that case (trash bags, fibers, and animal hairs) was one lone hair stuck to the young girl's thigh. The hair had characteristics that made it appear pubic-like but not enough to define *as* pubic. One thing was certain, however: The hair was not that of the young victim. Body hairs, especially pubic hairs, are a product of puberty and the hormones that flood the body during that phase of development. The victim, being prepubescent, could not have produced a hair with those traits. That information, gained through a microscopic examination of the hair, led to the hair being tested for mitochondrial DNA. The sequence of the hair was the same as the suspect in the case. Added to the other evidence stacked against him, he ultimately confessed to his brutal crime.

8

Fingerprints

From the early days of complicated body measurements to today's sophisticated biometric devices, the identification of individuals by their bodies has been a mainstay of government and law enforcement. Computerized databases now make it possible to compare thousands, or in the case of the FBI, *millions* of fingerprints in minutes.

THE "DISCOVERY" OF FINGERPRINTS

The recognition that fingerprints have value for forensic identification purposes is attributed to Dr. Henry Faulds. Faulds was born in Scotland and studied mathematics, logic, and the classics at Glasgow University. Later, he graduated with a physician's license from Anderson's College. Following his medical education, Faulds became a medical missionary for the Church of Scotland. He established a medical mission in Japan in 1874, with a hospital and a teaching facility. During a tour of an archaeological dig, Faulds noticed the finger marks of ancient craftsmen still in the ancient pottery fragments. Faulds did some informal research and became convinced that the patterns of ridges of fingertips were unique to each individual. At one point, his hospital was broken into; Faulds was sure that the suspect the police had in custody was innocent. In an attempt to exonerate the suspect, Faulds demonstrated that the fingerprints at the crime scene were different from those of the suspect. The police accepted Faulds' fingerprint "evidence" and released the man.

Faulds published his work on the use and classification of fingerprints in a letter to the scientific journal *Nature* in 1880. He returned to Britain in 1886 and presented the concept of fingerprint identification to Scotland Yard. Faulds's idea was rejected; he did not have enough data to support his assertions. Henry Faulds died in March 1930 at age 86, bitter that his contribution to fingerprinting had not been properly recognized.

The publication of Fauld's letter drew a quick response from William Herschel, a chief administrator from the Bengali British government office in India, who claimed that he, Herschel, and not Faulds had prior claim to the technique of fingerprints. Herschel had been using finger and palm prints to identify contractors in Bengal since the Indian Mutiny of 1857, employing a simplistic version of the system that Faulds eventually instituted some 40 years later. Herschel documented his own fingerprints over his lifetime to prove permanence. In fact, it may not have been Herschel's own idea to use prints for identification: The Chinese and Assyrians used prints as "signatures" at least since 9,000 years before the present, and the Indians had probably borrowed this custom. Herschel, however, did not mention their potential for forensic use, only bureaucratic record keeping.

Faulds and Herschel fought for many years, with Faulds demanding proof in 1894 that Herschel had ever used fingerprints officially. Herschel complied; years later, he wrote books and articles with variations of the argument that Faulds had cheated him of the credit he felt he was due. These books were published from 1905 onward, long after fingerprinting had come into widespread use.

THE NATURAL BORN CRIMINAL

Cesare Lombroso's theory of *l'umo delinquente*—the criminal man—influenced the entire history of criminal identification and criminology. Lombroso, an Italian physician of the late 1800s, espoused the idea that criminals "are evolutionary throwbacks in our midst. And these people are innately driven to act as a normal ape or savage would, but such behavior is considered criminal in our civilized society." He maintained that criminals could be identified because of their unattractive characteristics, with their external features reflecting their internal aberrations. While normal "civilized" people may occasionally commit crimes, the natural born criminal could not escape his mark.

Lombroso's comparison of criminals to apes made members of the lower classes and "foreigners" most similar to criminals. The "nature" of criminals was reflected in the structure of Lombroso's society. His list of criminal "traits" sounds laughable to us today: Criminals were said to have large jaws, larges faces, long arms, low and narrow foreheads, large ears, excess hair, darker skin, insensitivity to pain, and an inability to blush. It is easy to see from the racial stereotypes of Lombroso's description how society's "others" were automatically identified as criminal.

The idea of identifying "natural born killers" caught the attention of many anthropologists and law enforcement officials in the late 1800s, and even though Lombroso's work was later repudiated (many of his assertions were not supported by objective data), it spawned a great deal of activity in the search for real, measurable traits that would assist the police in identifying criminals. As discussed in chapter 2, a French police clerk named Alphonse Bertillon devised a complex system of anthropometric measurements, photographs, and a detailed description (what he called a *portrait parlé*) in 1883; it was later to be called Bertillonage (Ber-TEE-yon-ahj), after its inventor. At that time, the body was considered to be constant and, as Lombroso's work then maintained, reflective of one's inner nature. Bertillon's system was devised to quantify the body; by his method, Bertillon hoped to identify criminals as they were arrested and booked for their transgressions. Repeat offenders, who today would be called career criminals or recidivists, were at that time considered a particular problem to European police agencies. The growing capitals and cities of Europe allowed for certain anonymity, and criminals were free to travel from city to city, country to country, changing their names along the way as they plied their illegal trades. Bertillon hoped that his new system would allow the identification of criminals no matter where they appeared and, thus, help authorities keep track of undesirables.

Bertillonage was considered the premier method of identification for at least two decades—despite its limitations. The entire Bertillonage of a person was a complicated and involved process requiring an almost obsessive attention to detail. This made it difficult to standardize and, therefore, replicate accurately. Bertillon often lamented the lack of skill he saw in operators he himself had not trained. If the way the measurements were taken varied, then the same person might not be identified as such by two different operators. The *portrait parlé* added distinctive descriptors to aid the identification process, but here again the adjectives lacked precise objective definitions. "Lips might be 'pouting', 'thick', or 'thin', 'upper' or 'lower prominent', with 'naso-labial height great' or 'little' with or without a 'border'," writes Simon Cole, quoting from Bertillon's own instruction manual. What was meant by pouting, prominent, or little was better defined in Bertillon's mind than in the manual.

Bertillonage was used across Britain and in its colonies, especially India. The officials in the Bengal office—where Herschel worked—were

A class on fingerprinting at the FBI Academy *(Bettmann/Corbis)*

concerned with its utility, however. They wondered whether Bertillonage could distinguish individuals within the Indian population. Another concern the Bengali officials had with Bertillonage was the inconsistency between operators.

There were variations in the way operators took the measurements: Some rounded the results up, some rounded them down, and some operators even decided which measurements were to be taken and which ones could be ignored. Staff in the Bengal office even attempted to solve the variance problem by mechanizing the system! All of these variances made searches tedious, difficult, and ultimately prone to error, defeating the point of using the method. The problem became so extreme that the Bengal office dropped Bertillonage entirely except for one small component of the system: fingerprints. This begged for a way to classify fingerprints systematically—the limiting factor in the adoption of any identification system. Bertillonage was too cumbersome and finicky to systematize for quick sorting, as were photographs. Additionally, with the growing number of individuals who were being logged into police records, any system of identification had to be able to handle hundreds, thousands, and eventually thousands of thousands of records quickly, correctly, and remotely.

Sir Francis Galton, half-cousin of Charles Darwin, was an English Victorian anthropologist and statistician. Galton studied fingerprints as a type of anthropological measure of the human race; today, this type of study is called dermatoglyphics. Galton was the first to treat fingerprints as a quantitative problem and to apply statistics to the question of uniqueness. He studied the heritability and racial differences in fingerprints. Galton was the first to lay a scientific foundation for fingerprints, which assisted its acceptance in courts of law.

FINGERPRINTING IN THE UNITED STATES

The first known systematic use of fingerprint identification in the United States occurred in 1902 in New York City. Two years earlier, the New York Civil Service Commission had faced a scandal when several job applicants were discovered to have hired better educated persons to take their civil service exams for them. The New York Civil Service Commission therefore began fingerprinting applicants to verify their identity for entrance exams and to prevent better qualified persons taking tests for unscrupulous applicants. The first set of fingerprints was taken on December 19, 1902—the first use of fingerprints by a government agency in the United States.

Also in 1902, officials from the New York State Prison Department and the New York State Hospital traveled to England to study the fingerprint system there. The following year, the New York State prison system began to use fingerprints for the identification of criminals. The use of fingerprinting increased even more when the U.S. penitentiary in Leavenworth, Kansas, established a fingerprint bureau; this was the first use of fingerprints for criminal identification in the United States. During the 1904 World's Fair in St. Louis, John K. Ferrier of Scotland Yard taught the techniques and methods of fingerprinting to the public and law enforcement. Because of the fair's notoriety and the novelty of fingerprints as a "modern" method, public and professional awareness of fingerprinting was greatly enhanced in the United States.

The first U.S. criminal conviction using fingerprint evidence occurred in Chicago, in the case of Thomas Jennings, who was also tried for the crime of murdering Charles Hiller during a burglary; he was ultimately convicted in 1911. The International Association for Identification (IAI) was formed in 1915 initially as a professional association for "Bertillon clerks," but as fingerprinting grew and eventually replaced Bertillonage, the focus of the IAI also changed. *The Finger Print Instructor,* by Frederick Kuhne, was published in 1916; it is considered the first authoritative textbook on fingerprinting in the United States.

The growing need for a national repository and clearinghouse for fingerprint records led to an act of Congress on July 1, 1921, that established the Identification Division of the FBI in Washington, D.C., in 1924. A boost to the noncriminal use of fingerprinting came in 1933 when the U.S. Civil Service Commission (now the Office of Personnel Management) submitted more than 140,000 government employee and applicant fingerprints to the FBI's Identification Division. This prompted the FBI to establish a Civil Identification Section, whose fingerprint files would eventually expand well beyond the Criminal Files Section. In 1992, the Identification Division was renamed the Criminal Justice Information Services Division (CJIS); it is now housed in Clarksburg, West Virginia.

WHAT ARE FRICTION RIDGES?

Friction ridges appear on the palms and soles and on the ends of the fingers and toes; they are found on all primates (humans, apes, monkeys, and prosimians). In primates with prehensile tails ("finger-like" tails, such as on spider monkeys), friction ridges also appear on the volar surface of the tails. All primates have an arboreal evolutionary heritage: Trees have been and continue to be the primary habitat for most apes and monkeys, and humans share this arboreal heritage. Primates' hands and feet show adaptations for locomotion and maneuvering in the branches of trees. The opposable thumb provides a flexible and sturdy means of grasping branches or the food that hangs from them. Primates, unlike other mammals such as squirrels or cats, have nails instead of claws at the distal end of their phalanges. Claws would get in the way of grasping a branch (imagine making a fist with two-inch [5-cm] nails) and would provide insufficient structure to hold an animal with a high body weight (a one-pound squirrel is highly maneuverable in a tree, but a 150-pound jaguar is not). The ridges on the palms and soles provide friction between the grasping mechanism and whatever it grasps. Without them, it would be nearly impossible to handle objects in our environment.

Friction ridges develop in the womb and remain the same throughout life, barring any scarring or trauma to the deep-skin layer. This deep-skin layer acts as a template for the configuration of the friction ridges seen on the surface of the skin. Although people grow and increase in size, the patterns of the friction ridges on our bodies—which became permanent and fixed from about 17 weeks of embryonic development—do not change like other parts of our bodies.

What Is a Friction Ridge Print Made Of?

A friction ridge print is a representation of a friction ridge pattern in some medium. Friction ridge prints can be classified as either patent, if they are visible with the unaided eye, or latent, if they require some sort of assistance to make them visible. Patent prints can appear because of some transferable material on the ridge pattern, such as liquid blood, liquid paint, or dust, or because the ridge pattern was transferred to a soft substrate that had "memory" and retained the impression, like clay, fresh paint, or putty.

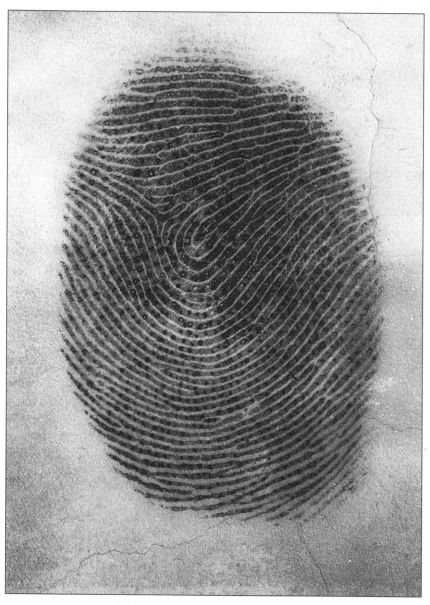

Not all friction ridge patterns are obvious, and some require physical, chemical, or optical enhancements to make them visible. The oldest and most common method is to use one or more fingerprint powders to create contrast between the ridge pattern and the background; black is the most commonly used color powder. *(Robert Llewellyn/Corbis)*

Latent prints are composed of the sweat and oils of the body that are transferred from the ridge pattern to some substrate where they persist for some time until found by one of numerous visualizing techniques. The most familiar visualizing technique is the use of fingerprint powder—colored, fluorescent, or magnetic materials that are very finely ground—which is brushed lightly over a suspected print to produce contrast between the background and the now-visible print.

Not all friction ridge patterns are patently obvious, and some require physical, chemical, or optical enhancements to make them visible. The oldest and still most common method is to use one or more fingerprint powders to create contrast between the ridge pattern and the background. These powders typically are available in black, white, and other colors, including metallic. Black is the most popular color because it creates the most contrast on a white card, commonly used for filing and recording friction ridge prints. This provides a uniform medium for the comparison of black ridges of the questioned print to the black inked ridges of the known print.

Principles of Friction Ridge Analysis

Since Francis Galton's time, friction ridges have been considered unique—that is, no individual's friction ridges are identical to anyone else's. The concept of uniqueness is typically associated with the philosopher Gottfried Wilhelm Leibniz (1646–1716), who stated ".... for in nature there are never two beings which are perfectly alike and in which it is not possible to find an internal difference, or at least a difference founded upon an intrinsic quality." While it is one thing to understand all people and things are separate in space and time, it is quite another to prove it.

Galton was the first to attempt to calculate the likelihood of finding two friction ridge patterns that are the same. Numerous researchers have re-calculated this probability over the years by various calculations based on differing assumptions. However, they all indicate that the probability of any one particular fingerprint being duplicated is somewhere between 0.000000954 and 1.2×10^{-80}—(0.0 with 78 zeros and 12) all very small numbers indeed. Technically, even infinitesimal probabilities such as these are still *probabilities* and do not represent true uniqueness (which

Author	Probability Value for a Latent Print with *36* Minutiae	Probability Value for a Latent Print with *12* Minutiae
Francis Galton (1892)	1.45×10^{-11}	9.54×10^{-7}
Sir Edward Henry (1900)	1.32×10^{-23}	3.72×10^{-9}
Victor Balthazard (1911)	2.12×10^{-22}	5.96×10^{-8}
Hem Chandra (Bose) Boze (1917)	2.12×10^{-22}	5.96×10^{-8}
Bert Wentworth and Harris Hawthorne Wilder (1918)	6.87×10^{-62}	4.10×10^{-22}
Karl Pearson (1930, 1933)	1.09×10^{-41}	8.65×10^{-17}
T. J. Y. Roxburgh (1933)	3.75×10^{-47}	3.35×10^{-18}
Harold Cummins and Charles Midlo (1943)	2.22×10^{-63}	1.32×10^{-22}
Mitchell Trauring (1963)	2.47×10^{-26}	2.91×10^{-9}
Sia Ram Gupta (1968)	1.00×10^{-38}	1.00×10^{-14}
James Osterburg, et al. (1977)	1.33×10^{-27}	1.10×10^{-9}
David A. Stoney (1985)	1.20×10^{-80}	3.5×10^{-26}

Note: comparison of probability of a particular fingerprint configuration using different published models for 36 minutiae and 12 minutiae (matches involve full, not partial matches)

would be a probability of 1 in ∞) but the values are such that latent fingerprints, with sufficient minutiae, can be considered unique by the vast majority of forensic scientists and the courts.

Under low-power magnification, friction ridge patterns are studied for the kind, number, and location of various ridge characteristics or minutiae. As with many other types of forensic evidence, it is not merely the presence or absence of minutiae that makes a print unique: It is the *presence, kind, number,* and, especially, *arrangement* of those characteristics that create a one-of-a-kind pattern. When two or more prints are compared, it is a careful point-by-point study to determine if enough of the significant minutiae in the known print are present in the questioned print, with no relevant differences.

The majority of prints that are identified, resolved, and compared are partial prints, representing only a portion of the complete print pattern. A friction ridge print scientist must then determine if a partial print is suitable for comparison—that is, if the print has the necessary and sufficient information to allow a proper comparison. A partial print, or even a complete print for that matter, may be identifiable as such but be smudged, too grainy, or too small for the scientist to make an accurate and unbiased comparison. Often this is the crucial step in a friction ridge print examination that is dependent on the scientist's experience, visual acuity, and judgment.

CLASSIFYING FINGERPRINTS

The patterning and permanency of friction ridges allows for their classification. As discussed earlier, the fact that fingerprints could be systematically sorted and cataloged was a main reason for their widespread adoption among government agencies. But it is important to keep in mind that it is the general patterns, and not the individualizing elements, that allow for this organization.

The first person to describe a taxonomy of fingerprints was Dr. Jan Purkyně, a Czech physician and one of the historical giants in the field of physiology. In 1823, Dr. Purkyně lectured on friction ridges in humans and primates and described a system of nine different basic ridge patterns. Today, all fingerprints are divided into three classes: loops, arches, and whorls. Loops have one or more ridges entering from one side of the print, curving back on themselves and exiting the fingertip on the same side. If the loop enters and exits on the side of the finger toward the little finger, it is called an ulnar loop; if the loop enters and exits on the side toward the thumb, it is termed a radial loop. All loops are surrounded by two diverging ridges called type lines; the point of divergence is called a delta because of its resemblance to a river delta and the Greek letter Δ (delta). The central portion of the loop is called the core.

Arches are the rarest of the three main classes of patterns. Arches are either plain, with ridges entering one side of the finger, gradually

Loops may be radial or ulnar, depending on the side of the hand to which the loop opens. *(Courtesy of the FBI, Government Printing Office; The Science of Fingerprints)*

rising to a rounded peak and exiting the other side; or tented, with a pronounced, sharp peak. A pattern that resembles a loop but lacks one of the required traits to be classified as a loop can also be designated as a tented arch. Arches do not have type lines, cores, or deltas.

Whorls are subdivided into plain whorl, central pocket loop, double loop, and accidental, as depicted. All whorls have type lines and at least two deltas. Central pocket loops and plain whorls have a minimum of one ridge that is continuous around the pattern, but it does not necessarily have to be in the shape of a circle; it can be an oval, an ellipse, or even a spiral. Plain whorls are located between the two deltas of the whorl pattern and central pocket loops are not located between the two deltas. This difference can be easily determined by drawing a line equidistant between the two deltas: If the line touches the circular core, then the whorl is a plain whorl; if not, it is a central pocket loop.

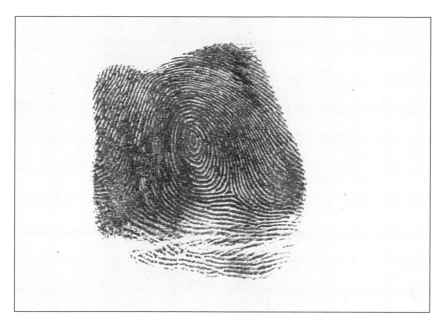

A whorl has a complicated definition, at least at first glance. It consists of one or more ridges that make or tend to make a complete circuit. The whorl has two deltas, and if one draws a line between them, it will touch at least one recurring ridge within the pattern. *(Courtesy of the FBI, Government Printing Office; The Science of Fingerprints)*

A double loop is made up of two loops that swirl around each other. Finally, an accidental is a pattern that combines two or more patterns (excluding the plain arch) and/or does not clearly meet the criteria for any of the other patterns.

CLASSIFICATION

The modern system of fingerprint classification is based on a system devised by Sir Edward Henry, which could process a maximum of 100,000 sets of prints. Henry, born in London, was a clerk for Lloyds of London and prepped to work in the Indian Civil Service. Appointed Inspector-General of Police in Bengal in 1891, Henry had already exchanged letters with Galton about fingerprinting and identification of criminals. Fingerprints had been common in the Bengal office as a means of identification for 40 years, having been introduced by Herschel. The police, however, did not use the method, and no easy

Arches can come in two types: plain or tented. An arch has no delta. The ridges enter the pattern from one side, peak, and dip to exit the opposite side. This is a plain arch. *(Courtesy of the FBI, Government Printing Office;* The Science of Fingerprints*)*

system of categorization was available. Henry and coworkers developed a method that quickly categorized fingerprints and allowed them to be easily organized and searched.

Henry's monograph *Classification and Uses of Fingerprints* was published in 1897 and was quickly adopted by other police forces. Henry's system was based on a calculation that encoded the general characteristics of a set of prints stored on a card, called ten print cards. Each ten print card was tagged with attributes that can vary from 1/1 to 32/32.

The modern fingerprint classification, based on Henry's original design, consists of a primary classification that encodes fingerprint pattern information into two numbers derived as follows. All arches and loops are considered "non-numerical" patterns and are given a value of zero. Whorls are given values depending on which finger they appear:

VALUES FOR FINGERS IN THE HENRY CLASSIFICATION SYSTEM

Right thumb, right index	16
Right middle, right ring	8
Right little, left thumb	4
Left index, left middle	2
Left ring, left little	1

Note: the values are summed, with one added to both groups, and the resulting primary classification is displayed like a fraction:

$$\frac{\text{R index} + \text{R ring} + \text{L thumb} + \text{L middle} + \text{L little} + 1}{\text{R thumb} + \text{R middle} + \text{R little} + \text{L index} + \text{L ring} + 1}$$

If, for example, all of an individual's fingers had whorls, the formula would look like:

$$16+8+4+2+1+1/16+8+4+2+1+1 = 32/32;$$

If all of their fingers had arches or loops instead, the formula would be:

$$0+0+0+0+0+1/0+0+0+0+0+1 = 1/1$$

In and of itself, a primary classification is class evidence. The primary classification was originally devised to sort individuals into smaller, more easily searched, categories; this, of course, was when fingerprints were searched by hand rather than by computer. Additional subdivisions of the classification scheme may be used, but they still only serve as a sieve through which to organize and efficiently search through filed prints. Comparison of minutiae and higher level details is the only method for fingerprint identification.

The problem with storing and sorting fingerprints using only the Henry-FBI classification system is that while the system stores all 10 prints as a set, rarely are full sets of fingerprints found at a crime scene. To search through even a moderately sized database of 10 print sets for an individual print would take too long and be too prone to error. Many agencies used to keep single-print files that contained the separate fingerprints of only the most frequent locally repeating criminals.

AUTOMATED FINGERPRINT IDENTIFICATION SYSTEMS (AFIS)

The advent of computers heralded a new age for many forensic sciences, and among the first to utilize the technology was the science of fingerprints. Capturing, storing, searching, and retrieving fingerprints via computer is now a standard occurrence among police agencies and forensic science laboratories. An automated fingerprint identification system, or AFIS (pronounced "AYE-fis"), are computerized data bases of digitized fingerprints that are searchable through software. An AFIS can store millions of prints that can be searched in a matter of minutes by a single operator. The core of this electronic system is a standard format developed by the FBI and the National Institute of Standards and Technology (NIST), with the advice of the National Crime Information Center (NCIC), which provides for the conversion of fingerprints into electronic data and their subsequent exchange via telecommunications and computers. Previously, although the data format was standard, the software and computers that operate AFIS were not, and several vendors offered products to law enforcement and forensic science agencies. The drawback was that these products were not compatible with each other, precluding the easy exchange of information between systems.

This situation began to change in 1999 when the FBI developed and implemented a new automated fingerprint system known as the Integrated Automated Fingerprint Identification System, or IAFIS (pronounced "EYE-aye-fis"). Although IAFIS is primarily a 10-print system for searching an individual's fingerprints like a standard AFIS, it can also digitally capture latent prints and 10-print images, in addition to doing the following:

- enhance an image to improve its quality

- compare crime-scene fingerprints against known 10-print records retrieved from the data base

- search crime-scene fingerprints against known fingerprints when no suspects have been developed

- automatically search the prints of an arrestee against a database of unsolved cases

Other advances are being made to solve the problem of noncompatible AFIS computers. The Universal Latent Workstation is the first in a new generation of interoperable fingerprint workstations. Several state and local agencies, the FBI, NIST, and AFIS technology manufacturers are developing standards to provide for the interoperability and sharing of fingerprint identification services. The workstation is part of that program and assists agencies and manufacturers understand and develop the concept of "encode once and search anywhere." The workstation allows agencies to enter data into the format of the system they purchased and use but also to share that data with other previously incompatible systems. Agencies will eventually be able to use this type of workstation to search local, state, neighboring, and FBI IAFIS systems, all with a single entry.

HOW LONG DO FRICTION RIDGE PRINTS LAST?

Plastic prints will last as long as the impressed material remains structurally intact. A print left in a medium such as blood or dust is quite fragile and does not last very long. Latent prints, however, can last for years if in the proper environments. Therefore, the age of a set of fingerprints is almost impossible to determine.

ELIMINATION PRINTS

As with any other type of evidence, obtaining known samples for elimination purposes can be of great assistance to the forensic scientist. These may not only eliminate individuals from an investigation's focus, they can also demonstrate a proper scientific mindset through a comprehensive series of comparisons. If these elimination knowns are incorporated into a trial presentation, they can create confidence in the mind of the trier of fact that not only do the defendant's known prints match, but the other potential subjects' prints do *not* match. Displaying what is and is not a match can clarify for the layperson the forensic scientist's process of identification and comparison.

9

Firearms Examination

Firearms examination is one of the key services that a forensic science laboratory provides. Even smaller laboratories with only a few employees will probably have a firearms examiner. Many crimes are committed with a firearm, to coerce cooperation or directly harm, and society has judged this implied or actual violence to be a severe crime. Firearms examination is complex, technical, detailed—and experiencing a renaissance with the development and growth of automated database searches. This computerization promises to revolutionize the nature of firearms examination and, perhaps, forensic science.

In 1863, during the U.S. Civil War, Confederate general Stonewall Jackson was fatally wounded on the battlefield. The deadly projectile was excised from his body and, through examination of its size and shape, determined to be 0.67-caliber ball ammunition. This was not the 0.58-caliber minié ball used by the Union army but ammunition typical of the Confederate forces. Jackson had been shot by one of his own soldiers! A few years later, in 1876, a Georgia state court allowed the testimony of an expert witness on the topic of firearms analysis.

These are the first examples of firearms analysis and testimony in the United States.

The field of forensic firearms examination is sometimes referred to as *ballistics* or *forensic ballistics*. This terminology is not wholly accurate: Ballistics is the study of an object in flight and is under the domain of physics. Forensic ballistics may be somewhat more accurate, but it does not capture what forensic firearms examiners do in their job. They certainly are not analyzing the trajectories of bullets *while* they are in flight! Many of the principles, equations, and methodologies of ballistics are used, for example, to reconstruct a shooting incident. But the discipline of forensic firearms science is more than that: It encompasses the study of firearms and their manufacture, operation, and performance; the analysis of ammunition and its by-products (such as muzzle-to-target distance and gunshot residue); and the individualizing characteristics that are transferred from firearms to bullets and cartridge cases.

TYPES OF FIREARMS

Generally, firearms can be divided into two types: handguns and shoulder firearms. The former class includes revolvers and pistols, while the latter is more diverse, encompassing rifles, shotguns, machine guns, and submachine guns. A broad knowledge and familiarity with the various types, makes, models, and styles of firearms are crucial to being a successful forensic firearms scientist. This should not only cover new products as they emerge on the market but also older models and the history of manufacturers and their products.

Handguns are firearms that are fired with one hand. These appear in two major types: revolvers and semiautomatic pistols. A revolver is a handgun that feeds ammunition into the firing chamber by means of a revolving cylinder. The cylinder can swing out to the side or be hinged to the frame and released by a latch or a pin for loading and unloading. A single-action revolver requires that the hammer be cocked each time it is fired; a double-action revolver can be cocked by hand or by the pulling of the trigger that also rotates the cylinder.

A semiautomatic pistol, on the other hand, feeds ammunition by means of a spring-loaded vertical magazine. Although the term *automatic* is often applied to pistols fed by magazines, they are not truly

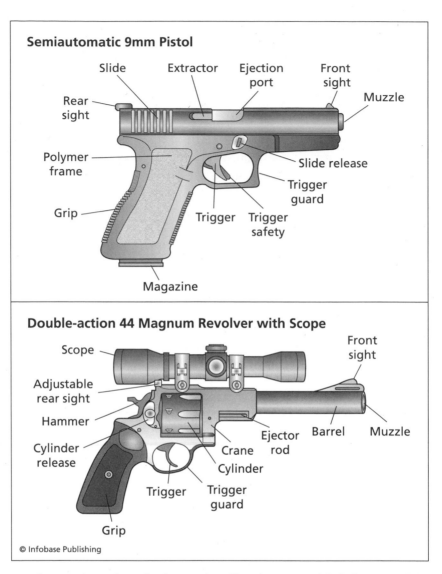

Revolvers and pistols are both considered handguns. *(Modeled after artwork by Erik Dahlberg; www.FirearmsID.com)*

automatic in their firing. An automatic firearm is one that continues to fire ammunition while the trigger is depressed; a semiautomatic firearm fires one bullet for each pull of the trigger. When fired, semiautomatic pistols use the energy of the recoil and the sliding of the breech block

Bolt-action Rifle with Scope

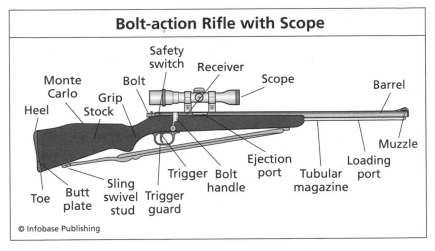

Shoulder arms consist of rifles, automatic rifles, machine guns, and shotguns. *(Modeled after artwork by Erik Dahlberg; www.FirearmsID.com)*

(slide) or the recoil of the cartridge to expel the empty cartridge from the firearm and load a live round into the firing chamber. Springs are used to store the energy and expend it.

Shoulder arms consist of rifles, automatic rifles, machine guns, and shotguns. Rifles are fired from the shoulder with two hands. Rifles may be single-shot, repeating, semiautomatic, or automatic. A single-shot rifle must be loaded and fired, the cartridge extracted, and then reloaded. Such rifles were common as a young boy's first firearm just after the turn of the century but are almost nonexistent now. Repeating rifles fire one bullet with each pull of the trigger, but the expended cartridge must be expelled, cocked, and reloaded from a magazine manually. Repeating rifles may be bolt-action (like an M1 seen in many war films or hunting rifles) or lever-action (made popular in cowboy films). Semiautomatic rifles use the energy of the fired ammunition to expel the empty cartridge, cock the firing mechanism, and reload a live round. Thus, one pull of the trigger fires one round, and this may be done sequentially until the magazine is empty. Assault rifles, like the AK-47 or M-16, can be fired either like semiautomatic rifles or in automatic mode: Pull the trigger, and the firearm will fire ammunition continuously until all the ammunition is gone. A machine gun is a fully automatic firearm and therefore is fed ammunition from a high-capacity belt or box. Because of their size and the strength of the recoil, machine guns are fired from a tripod or other mounted/fixed position. A submachine gun is a machine gun fired while held in the hands.

FIREARM BARRELS

The interior surface of the barrels of the firearms discussed thus far (handguns and rifles, but not shotguns) are rifled with a series of ridges and valleys, respectively called lands and grooves, which spiral the length of barrel. The lands dig into the bullet surface as it travels down the barrel, imparting spin to stabilize the bullet's flight once it leaves the barrel. This creates land and groove impressions on the bullet surface as well as impressions of the microscopic imperfections of the interior barrel surface called striations, or striae.

During the manufacture of a barrel, a hole is drilled down the length of a steel bar of the proper size for the intended firearm. The grooves are

Lands and grooves in the barrel help to stabilize the bullet during flight. *(Courtesy of Alliance Forensic Laboratory, Inc.)*

cut into the barrel by either a large segmented tool, called a broach, or a rifling button—a stiff metal rod with a flanged tip—which is run down the length of the hole. When the grooves are cut, they are cut in a spiral of a certain direction or twist (right-handed/clockwise or left-handed/counterclockwise); this is what spins the bullet and creates a stable flight path. Some manufacturers produce barrels with four grooves, some with five or six, depending on the design and desired performance of the firearm.

The interior, or bore diameter, of a rifled barrel is the diameter of a circle that touches the tops of the lands. The caliber of a firearm used to mean the same thing as bore diameter but now refers mostly to the size of a particular ammunition cartridge; firearms, however, are still referred to in their nominal caliber. A barrel's internal diameter is an exact measurement, while caliber is an approximation: The barrel of a .38 firearm may actually measure between 0.345 and 0.365 inches (also note that calibers do not use the zero before the decimal). The caliber of American and British ammunition is typically measured in inches, and all others are measured in millimeters (a Smith and Wesson .32 versus a Beretta 9 mm).

Shotguns can fire numerous projectiles, called pellets or "shot" of varying sizes; they may also fire single projectiles called slugs. A single-barrel shotgun can be either single-shot (manually loaded) or repeating-shot in design (with a spring-loaded auto feeder or manual pump feeder with a reservoir of three to five shells). The interior of a shotgun barrel is smooth so that nothing deflects or slows down the pellets as they

PELLET SIZE ORGANIZED NUMERICALLY

Pellet Size	Diameter (in inches)
9	0.08
8	0.09
7	0.10
6	0.11
5	0.12

traverse its length. The muzzle of a shotgun barrel may be constricted by the manufacturer to produce a choke, which helps to keep the pellets grouped longer once they leave the barrel. The influence of choke on the shot pattern increases with the distance the pellets travel; the range of a shotgun is short compared to rifles, but the choke can improve the chance of hitting targets at near-to-mid ranges. The choke may also be modified by barrel inserts.

The diameter of the shotgun barrel is called the gauge, and it is the number of lead balls with the same diameter as the barrel that would weigh 1 pound. For example, 12 lead balls, which together weigh 1 pound, have the same diameter as the interior of a 12-gauge shotgun (about 0.729 inch, or 18.5 mm). The exception to this system is the so-called 410-gauge shotgun, which has its bore diameter measured in inches (0.410 inch, or 10.4 mm).

ANATOMY OF AMMUNITION

Ammunition is what a firearm fires. It is typically a self-contained cartridge that is comprised of one or more projectiles, propellant (to act as fuel), and a primer (to ignite the propellant). As with firearms, ammunition comes in two major types: Bullets for handguns and rifles, and shells for shotguns.

Bullets, the first type of projectile, can be classified as lead (or lead alloy), fully jacketed, and semi-jacketed. Lead (alloy) bullets are pieces of lead hardened with minute amounts of other metals (such as antimony) and formed into the desired shape. Although hardened, they are too soft to use in most modern firearms other than .22 rifles or pistols. A fully jacketed bullet has a lead core that is encased in a harder material, usually copper-nickel alloys or steel. A semi-jacketed bullet has a metal jacket that covers only a portion of the bullet, with the nose often exposed. Because the nose of the bullet is softer than the surrounding jacket, the tip expands, or "mushrooms," on impact, transferring its energy to the target. A hollow-point bullet is a semi-jacketed bullet that has a hollowed-out tip to increase this effect. Some semi-jacketed bullets leave the base exposed but cover the tip; these have a greater penetrating power due to the hardness of the tip material and tend to pass through the target.

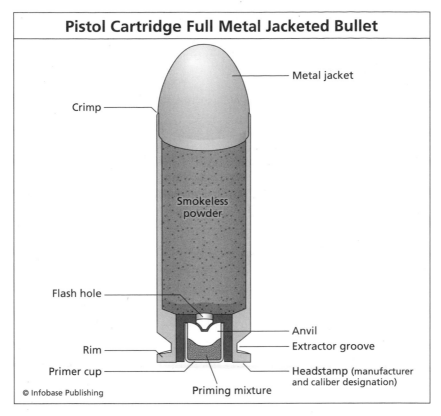

Pistol Cartridge Full Metal Jacketed Bullet

Metal jacket

Crimp

Smokeless powder

Flash hole

Anvil

Rim

Extractor groove

Primer cup

Headstamp (manufacturer and caliber designation)

Priming mixture

© Infobase Publishing

Ammunition is what a firearm fires; it is typically a self-contained cartridge that is composed of one or more projectiles, propellant (to act as fuel), and a primer (to ignite the propellant). *(Modeled after artwork by Erik Dahlberg; www. FirearmsID.com)*

Shotguns, as noted above, can fire pellets or slugs. Dozens of varieties of projectiles, from explosive bullets to "safety" ammunition consisting of pellets in a small sack to disable airline hijackers, are currently available and may be encountered in forensics casework.

The propellant is the fuel that propels the projectile down and out of the firearm's barrel. The most common propellant by far is smokeless powder, which was developed in response to the huge plumes of smoke black powder produces upon ignition. Smokeless powder is composed of cellulose nitrate combined with various chemicals to stabilize the mix and modify it for safe manufacture and transport.

The primer is what ignites the propellant. It consists of a small metal cup containing a percussion-sensitive material (it explodes on impact) that, when struck, creates enough heat to ignite the propellant. The small cup is set in place at the rear of the cartridge, where it is struck by the firing pin. Modern primer materials consist of lead styphnate, antimony sulfide, barium nitrate, and tetracene. Because of the concerns of toxicity over long-term exposure to law enforcement officers, many primers are now made from organic primers that are lead-free.

WHAT HAPPENS WHEN AMMUNITION IS DISCHARGED?

When the hammer strikes the primer cap on a live round chambered in a weapon, the primer explodes and ignites the propellant. The burning of the propellant generates hot gases, which expand and push the bullet from its cartridge case and down the barrel. The propellant is designed and the ammunition constructed so as to continue to burn: If the propellant stopped burning, the friction between the bullet and the rifling of the barrel would cause the bullet to stop. The friction between the bullet and the rifling also transfers the pattern of lands and grooves to the bullet's exterior. More importantly, it also transfers the microscopic striations—themselves transferred to the barrel's inner surface from the tool used to cut the lands and grooves—and these are used by the forensic firearms scientist in the microscopical comparison of known and questioned bullets.

If the firearm—a revolver, for example—retains the spent cartridge, then the only marks to be found on the cartridge that could be used for comparison would be the firing pin impression, the mark made by the firing pin as it strikes the primer cap. Firearms that expel the spent cartridge, however, may produce a variety of marks indicative of the method of cartridge extraction (extraction marks) and ejection (ejection marks) from the chamber. Other common marks left on a cartridge case during discharge are breech marks. The discharge of a firearm creates recoil, forcing the cartridge case backward into the firearm's breech face, the part that holds the base of the cartridge case in the chamber. Recoil causes the cartridge base to smack against the breech face, which receives an impression of any imperfections.

As the bullet leaves the barrel's muzzle, it is followed by a plume of the hot gases that forced it down the barrel. This plume contains a variety of materials, such as partially burned gunpowder flakes, microscopic molten blobs of the primer chemicals, the bullet, and the cartridge. As these materials strike, or come to rest on, a surface, they transfer potential evidence of that surface's distance from the firearm's muzzle and other materials that may indicate that surface's association with the firing of a firearm or one that has been fired.

BULLET COMPARISONS

Many published studies have demonstrated that no two firearms produce the same unique marks on fired bullets and cartridge cases; this is even true with firearms of the same make and model. The machining of the manufacturing process and the use of the firearm leave surface marks on its metal parts that are not reproducible in other firearms. These marks are transferred to the bullets and casings when discharged from the firearm.

Because there is no practical method of comparing the striations on the inner surface of a rifled weapon with the striations on a fired bullet, reference bullets of the same make, style, and caliber must be created by firing them from the questioned firearm. Not only would cutting the barrel open be impractical, but also the comparison would then be between positive (the barrel) and negative (the questioned bullet) impressions. The known fired bullets must be captured and preserved, however, so that they are as "pristine" as possible and not deformed or damaged. Firearms are typically discharged into a water tank where the water slows and eventually stops the bullet without altering its striations; other bullet recovery systems are used from the simple (a bucket filled with rubber shavings) to the high tech (sandwiched layers of specialized materials) The known bullet is then recovered, labeled, and used as a reference in the comparison; multiple known bullets may be created, if necessary.

The questioned and known bullets are first examined with the naked eye and slight magnification. The number of lands and grooves, their twist, and the bullets' weights are recorded. Because these are higher-order class characteristics, any deviations from the known bullet indicate

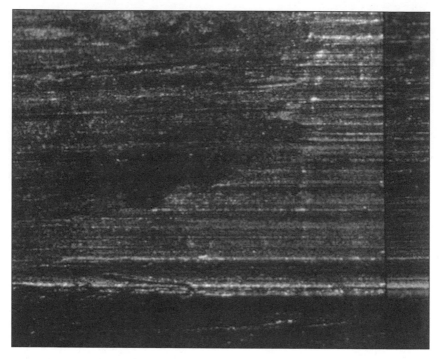

The two bullets must not be merely similar but must have the same striation patterns, with no significant differences. *(Courtesy of Alliance Forensics Laboratory, Inc.)*

that the two bullets were fired from different barrels. If the lands, grooves, and direction of twist all concur, then the next step is microscopic comparison of the striations on the bullets.

The comparison is performed on a comparison stereomicroscope with special stages that facilitate positioning the bullets in the focal plane and allow for rotation of the bullets on their long axis. The bullets are positioned on the stages, one on each, both pointing in the same direction, and held in position with clay or putty; this allows for easy repositioning, and the soft material will not mark the bullets' surfaces. The known bullet is positioned to visualize a land or groove with distinctive striations. The questioned bullet is then rotated until a land or groove, respectively, comes into view with the same striation markings. The lands and grooves of the two bullets must have the same widths. More importantly, the two bullets must not be merely similar but they must have the same striation patterns with no significant differences. This last point is critical: Not only must the forensic firearms scientist see the positive correlation between the significant information on the bullets' surfaces, he or she must also not see any unexplained differences. Each rifled barrel is unique: No two of them will have identical striation patterns. This is true even of barrels that have been rifled in succession, one after the other. It takes education, practice, and mentoring to train a person's eye and judgment on the subtleties of bullet striation patterns.

FIREARM DATABASES AND AUTOMATED SEARCH SYSTEMS

Whether a firearm is used by the same criminal or shared between members of a criminal enterprise, firearm evidence can link a person or persons to multiple crimes. The difficulty in doing so is searching and comparing numerous bullets or casings. If the crimes were committed across multiple jurisdictions, then the task becomes even more involved.

Two automated search engines were developed in the 1990s. DRUG-FIRE, developed by the FBI, analyzes cartridge casing markings. The other system, developed by Walsh Automation, Inc., in collaboration with the Bureau of Alcohol, Tobacco, and Firearms (ATF), is called the Integrated Ballistic Identification System (IBIS), which primarily analyzes bullet striations but also works with cartridge casings. The systems integrate digital imaging, novel data collection, computerized databases of images, and communications technology. Unfortunately, at the time they were established, the systems were not compatible with each other, and specialized hardware and software were needed for each.

In January 1996, the ATF and the FBI acknowledged the need for IBIS and DRUGFIRE to be compatible. This meant the systems had to capture an image according to a standard protocol and with a minimum quality standard and then exchange these images electronically so that an image captured on one system could be analyzed on the other. In June 1996, the National Institute of Standards and Technology (NIST) issued the minimal specifications for this data exchange. In May 1997, a board for the National Integrated Ballistics Information Network (NIBIN) was created, and in December 1999, the FBI and ATF formally established their roles in the network.

By 2002, the NIBIN program had expanded to 222 sites. When complete in all 16 multistate regions, NIBIN will be available at approximately 235 sites, covering every state and major population centers. Since the inception of this technology, more than 5,300 hits have been logged, providing investigative leads in many cases where none would otherwise exist.

10

Testimony and Report Writing

The culmination of a forensic scientist's efforts is to write a report on the examinations performed and then, if needed, to testify to those results in a court of law. If someone who was a notable scientist could not effectively testify to what he or she did or saw, that person would be a failure as a forensic scientist. A professional forensic scientist must be able to explain the theories, methods, procedures, analyses, results, and interpretations of the scientific examinations he or she performed. And this must be done objectively, without the scientist being an advocate for either side in a case. Impartiality is the hallmark of science, and this is especially true of forensic science, whether in a civil or a criminal case. It is important for the forensic scientist to be able to distinguish between the two and the responsibilities therein when it comes to preparing reports and delivering testimony.

CIVIL CASES

Civil cases usually involve private disputes between persons or organizations. Criminal cases involve an action that is considered to be harmful to society as a whole.

A civil case begins when a person or entity (such as a corporation or the government), called the plaintiff, claims that another person or entity, called the defendant, has failed to carry out a legal duty owed to the plaintiff. (Plaintiffs and defendants are also referred to as parties or litigants.) The plaintiff may ask the court to tell the defendant to fulfill the duty, or make compensation for the harm done, or both. Legal duties include respecting rights established under the Constitution or under federal or state law.

Civil suits are brought in both state and federal courts. An example of a civil case in a state court would be if a citizen (including a corporation) sued another citizen for not living up to a contract. Individuals, corporations, and the federal government can also bring civil suits in federal court that claim violations of federal statutes or constitutional rights. For example, the federal government can sue a hospital for overbilling Medicare and Medicaid, a violation of a federal statute. An individual could sue a local police department for violation of his or her constitutional rights—for example, the right to assemble peacefully.

CRIMINAL CASES

A person accused of a crime is generally charged in a formal accusation called an indictment (for felonies or serious crimes) or information (for misdemeanors). The government, on behalf of the people of the United States, prosecutes the case through the United States Attorney's Office if the person is charged with a federal crime. A state attorney's office prosecutes state crimes.

It is not the victim's responsibility to bring a criminal case. In a kidnapping case, for instance, the government would prosecute the kidnapper; the victim would not be a party to the action. In some criminal cases, there may not be a specific victim. For example, state governments arrest and prosecute people accused of violating laws against driving while intoxicated because society regards that as a serious offense that can result in harm to others.

When a court determines that an individual has committed a crime, that person will receive a sentence. The sentence may be an order to pay a monetary penalty (a fine and/or restitution to the victim), imprisonment, or supervision in the community (by a court employee called a

U.S. probation officer if a federal crime), or a combination of the three punishments.

WRITING A LABORATORY REPORT

A forensic science laboratory report may vary widely in its particular format but must contain the following information:

- the name of the examiner who conducted the tests

- the agency where the examiner works

- the date the report was issued

- the case identification information (laboratory number, case number, etc.)

- contact information for the examiner

- the items examined

- the methods and instrumentation used to examine and analyze the submitted items

- the results of the examinations and/or analyses

- any interpretations or statistics relevant to the results

- a statement of the disposition of the evidence

- the signatures of the examiner and any reviewers of the report (many laboratories require that signatures be notarized)

The format of the report should roughly follow that of a standard scientific paper: introduction, materials and methods, results, conclusions, and discussion. It is important to remember, however, that, unlike a scientific paper in a peer-reviewed journal, a forensic science laboratory report is *not* intended for other scientists. Most of the readers of a forensic science laboratory report are law enforcement officers, attorneys, and judges, all of whom may have little to no training in science. This requires a special effort to make the reports readable, intelligible, and concise while retaining the necessary information to maintain its scientific rigor.

To this end, forensic science laboratory reports should be *summations* of analyses, not complete and definitive scientific research results.

Science is a public endeavor, and articles are the canonical means of communicating original scientific results. By being published, they are meant for public scrutiny, both by the expert and the layperson. Scientific journal articles are formal communications, and from them one can legitimately infer the norms and values expressed in them to the standards by which the scientific community operates.

Scientific text has several features that distinguish it from other types of text. The *style* is the syntax of sentences or the choice of words used to communicate the materials and methods, the results, and the discussion of the research. The *presentation* is the way the text is organized and the data are displayed. Finally, the *argument* is the means employed to support the claims offered by the researchers.

Forensic laboratory reports differ from standard scientific articles published in journals in several important ways. These differences reflect the nature of forensic science and the requirements placed on its "science-ness" by the legal system.

A FORENSIC REPORT IS NOT A SCIENTIFIC REPORT

The 17th-century scientific report would hardly be recognizable to students and researchers today. The emphasis was on the scientist, not the science. The text, devoid of technical vocabulary, was written in a first-person narrative. Its credibility was gained through the scientist's reliable testimony of what he observed and experienced with his own senses. Facts took precedence over argument, but numerical data was noticeably lacking. Tables were the only means of expressing quantitative data. Plots or graphic presentations were not "invented" until late in the 18th century. Facts were bound by causation and not by theory; "A" caused "B" but not in any larger sense than that one-to-one relationship. Science was seen as a sort of museum, a storehouse of facts to be acquired, cataloged, and kept.

Twentieth-century scientific reports, by contrast, are heavy with technical vocabulary and focus on the relationships among sets of allied facts that are bound by theory. The article's structure does not vary with the whims of its author; it has headings, sections, references, and so on. In fact, the abstract—the condensation of the article that appears at the beginning of a scientific article—was not "standardized" until about 1920. Quantification is now the major contributor to one's impression of an article's objectivity, not the testimonial of the author's senses. The style is impersonal, in the third person, and free of adornments. Experiments are not the subject of the article in the 20th century: They are tools designed to produce results according to a theory. The argument is key—the data do not speak for themselves, as in the 17th century—and interpretations can be derived from data only through the power of a sound argument. This change can be explained by a list of factors:

- the increased complexity of science over the last few centuries,

- the accumulation of knowledge,

- the demand for higher standards of proof (personal experience is not enough), and

- the greater volumes of data (standardized structure makes it easier to read, "skim," and overview).

Forensic science reports as issued by laboratories exhibit a mixed style, combining aspects of the 17th- and 20th-century formats. Crime lab reports largely have a 20th-century presentation and argument style. Some forensic scientists argue that the facts speak for themselves, but in reality, without an interpretation ("the Q1 paint sample could have come from the suspect vehicle"), there is no expert opinion—the very reason a forensic scientist goes to court. In court, however, the report and the testimony take on a very 17th-century style. Experts testify to what they did and how they did it; a large part of their credibility comes from their professional experience.

Forensic science reports from different laboratories often have conflicting styles with no standard format. They are even dissimilar to the "standard" scientific article format: no abstract, no introduction, no materials and methods, and no references. Forensic reports should contain the following:

- name and address of the laboratory

- case identifier (number)

- name, address, and identifier of the contributor

- date of receipt of evidence

- date of report

- descriptive list of submitted evidence

- identification of the methodology

- identity and signature of examiner

- results and conclusions

The case file should contain documentation that supports the results and conclusions in the report. That documentation should include data obtained through the analytical process as well as information regarding the packaging of the evidence upon receipt and the condition of the evidence. All documentation generated during an examination must be preserved according to the written policy of the forensic laboratory, including paper, electronic files, standards, controls, observations, the results of the tests, charts, graphics, photographs, printouts, and communications.

Forensic laboratories review a percentage—and in some cases that is 100 percent—of cases prior to the report being issued. A case review should be conducted by a minimum of two personnel, and the review should consist of a technical review and an administrative review. A technical review should be conducted on the report, and the notes and data supporting the report must be reviewed independently by a technically competent peer. Once a report has been reviewed, initials or other appropriate markings must be maintained in the case file by the personnel conducting the review. An administrative review should be conducted on the report to ensure adherence to laboratory policy and editorial correctness. Laboratory administration will determine the course of action if an examiner and the reviewer fail to agree.

TESTIMONY

While science is a public endeavor, police investigations are often a matter of discretion. Scientists are accustomed to scrutiny by other scientists and the public. Forensic scientists also face scrutiny in courtroom by the attorneys, the jury, and the judge. But not every case that a forensic scientist works on will go to trial. In fact, opportunities for testifying may be infrequent and irregular. A case may not go to trial for a number of reasons: The defendant may enter a guilty plea, a plea arrangement may be made for a lesser sentence, the attorney may decide the evidence is not needed for trial, or the charges may be dropped.

The first notice that a forensic scientist will be required for testimony will often be a subpoena, an official request from the court that he or she appears before it. The word is Latin for "under penalty," and if a subpoena is ignored, the scientist may face jail or additional penalties. The subpoena states the defendant's name, the jurisdiction, the date and time the scientist is requested to appear, and contact information for the requesting attorney.

When forensic scientists step into a courtroom to testify, they are, in essence, entering a foreign realm where only some of the rules of science apply. As M. Lee Goff, a noted forensic entomologist, describes it in his book *A Fly for the Prosecution* (2000):

> Academics and the legal system do not usually coexist in comfort. The laws of science and the rules of evidence have little in common. In theory, Academia functions on the principle of collegiality. In theory and reality, the American legal system is adversarial. The average academic entering the legal system is in for a tremendous culture shock.

The legal arena has its own rules. Most, but not all, apply to experts, and they must abide by the rules. Experts have leeway in the courtroom that no other witnesses have. It is a strange intersection between science and the law where even words have different meanings. Take for example the word *error*. To a scientist, an error is something that occurs naturally in all measurements and is accounted for in the statistics that are generated, such as "standard error of the mean." Errors, in science, cannot be avoided and are reported in due process. An attorney, on the other hand, hears the word *error* and thinks: *Mistake!* The scientist has just admitted to doing something wrong, in the lawyer's view, and has opened the door for further questioning. This clash of cultures does not always serve either side very well and may obscure what both parties seek.

When a forensic scientist testifies, he or she does so as an expert witness—that is, someone who knows more about a topic or subject than the average person. The scientist is brought to court by either the prosecution or defense and offered as an expert in some area of study that will aid the judge or jury (the trier of fact, as explained in chapter 3) in reaching their verdict. The scientist then undergoes a process of establishing his or her education, training, experience, and expertise in that discipline; this process is called voir dire (pronounced "vwa deer"). Old French for "speak the truth." Voir dire is a process where the attorneys, and occasionally the judge, question the scientist about his or her education, training, and experience. The scientist will often need to cite his educational degrees, work history, previous testimony experience, publications, professional associations, and other relevant information that will justify her expertise to the court. The attorney offering the scientist as an expert asks questions that will lay a foundation for the scientist's credentials; the opposing attorney then asks questions that may confirm or weaken that foundation. It is important for the scientist to provide *relevant* qualifications to the court. For example, being coach of the local high school soccer team has no bearing on whether someone should be considered an expert in drug analysis.

If the court rules that the scientist does possess sufficient credentials, then he or she may testify on that subject in the case at hand. The scientist must be careful to remain within the bounds of his or her expertise. It may be tempting for the scientist to answer questions at the margin of his experience and offer speculative answers to be helpful or sound authoritative—*but he should not do it!* Few things will reduce a forensic scientist's expertise in the jury's minds faster than exceeding expertise. It is better for an expert to answer truthfully, "I don't know" than to exceed his or her limits of knowledge, training, or experience.

Ordinary witnesses may only testify to what they have directly experienced through their five senses. This testimony must be factual in nature, and the witness, in nearly all cases, is barred from offering opinions, conjectures, or hypothetical information. Unlike other types of witnesses, however, expert witnesses are allowed to offer their opinions about evidence or situations that fall within their area of expertise. These opinions are allowed because the scientist is an expert in that area and knows more than anyone else in the courtroom about that topic;

his or her opinion and expertise will assist the trier of fact in deciding the case.

Scientific evidence can be powerful. It can also be suspect. Judges and juries may ignore an expert's opinion evidence because it is just that: the expert's view on that issue. Often, however, those opinions and views are based on solid scientific data generated through valid analyses and therefore have a firm basis in fact. Expert witnesses must always tread a fine line between their science and the potential for advocacy in a case.

Conclusion

The noted historian Robert J. Shafer notes the following in his *A Guide to Historical Method* (3rd edition, 1980):

[T]he historian endeavors to control his data by a careful search for all possibly significant information. . . . This understanding must involve a selection of the evidence and its synthesis into an account. Complete knowledge of complex human events appears to be nearly impossible. Still, the investigator can aspire to sufficient knowledge to permit an explanation or interpretation of the data in which we can have considerable confidence. The value of the interpretation depends on the availability of adequate data, the condition of the sources and the availability and reliability of the witnesses, and on the methodological or disciplinary training of the investigator who gathers and evaluates the data.

In this explanation of history, one hears the echoes of the perspective of forensic science offered in this volume. Criminal investigators aspire to obtain sufficient knowledge through their questioning, collection of evidence, and its analysis, in order to permit an interpretation of events with considerable confidence. How much evidence is collected, how well it is preserved and analyzed, the training and expertise of the analysts, and the quality of the methods all go into the "final solution." *Science versus Crime* is intended to provide a glimpse into the mindset and the tools used to solve crimes with science.

This book's introduction ends with a Sherlock Holmes quote. In another Holmes story, "The Sign of Four," Holmes notes to Watson that a French detective, Francois le Villard, "possesses two out of three qualities necessary for the ideal detective. He has the power of observation and that of deduction. He is only wanting in knowledge." With *Science versus Crime,* the beginning scientific detective, no matter what his or her age, will not be wanting for that knowledge.

CHRONOLOGY

1810 François-Eugène Vidocq, a noted wily criminal, makes a deal with the Paris police to become an informant in Paris's toughest prison rather than being sent to the galleys. Vidocq would eventually establish the first detective force, the Sûreté of Paris.

1828 Scottish physicist and geologist William Nicol invents the polarizing light microscope, revolutionizing the study of microscopic materials.

1835 Belgian mathematician and statistician Adolphe Quételet, who based his work on the criminology of Cesare Lombroso, postulates that no two human bodies are exactly alike.

London policeman Henry Goddard performs the first forensic bullet comparison. Goddard's work implicates a butler who faked a burglary to commit murder based on similar flaws in a questioned bullet and the mold that made it.

1838 William Stewart of Baltimore murders his father and is convicted based on bullet evidence, making it the first case solved by forensic firearms examination in the United States.

1858 Sir William Herschel, a British officer working for the Indian Civil Service, uses fingerprints on documents to verify document signatures, a practice recognized in India but not forensically.

1863 German scientist Christian Schönbein discovers the oxidation of hydrogen peroxide when exposed to hemoglobin. The foaming reaction is the first presumptive test for blood.

1880 Henry Faulds, a Scottish physician working in Tokyo, publishes a paper in the journal *Nature* suggesting that fingerprints could identify an individual involved in a crime. Faulds goes on to use fingerprints to solve a burglary.

1883 Parisian police clerk Alphonse Bertillon identifies his first recidivist (habitual criminal) based on his system of anthropometry.

1887 British physician Arthur Conan Doyle publishes his first Sherlock Holmes story.

1891 Austrian magistrate and criminalistics pioneer Hans Gross publishes *Handbuch fur Untersuchungsrichter* (Handbook for examining magistrates), the first comprehensive text to promote the use of science and microscopy to solve crimes.

1892 British polymath Francis Galton publishes *Fingerprints,* the first text on the nature of fingerprints and their use as a forensic method.

1894 Captain Alfred Dreyfus of France is convicted of treason based on a faulty handwriting identification by Alphonse Bertillon.

1896 London police commissioner Edward Henry develops a classification system for fingerprints that becomes the standard taxonomy in Europe and North America.

1901 Edward Henry is appointed head of Scotland Yard and pushes for the adoption of fingerprints over Bertillon's anthropometry.

Austrian physician Karl Landsteiner discovers human blood groups, which he classifies into the ABO system in 1909. He will be awarded the Nobel Prize in physiology or medicine for his work in 1930. Landsteiner's work on blood forms the basis of nearly all subsequent forensic blood work.

1902 Dr. Henry P. DeForrest pioneers the first systematic use of fingerprinting in the United States, for applicants to the New York Civil Service Commission.

Professor R. A. Reiss, a professor at the University of Lausanne, Switzerland, and a student of Alphonse Bertillon, pioneers academic curricula in forensic science.

1903   The New York State prison system begins the systematic use of fingerprints in the United States for criminal identification.

At Leavenworth Federal Penitentiary, Kansas, Will West, a new inmate, is initially confused with a resident convict, William West, through the use of anthropometry. They are later found to be easily differentiated by their fingerprints.

1908   U.S. president Theodore Roosevelt establishes a special investigations division, subsequently known as the Federal Bureau of Investigation (FBI).

1910   With Marcelle Lambert, Victor Balthazard, professor of forensic medicine at the Sorbonne, Paris, publishes the first comprehensive hair study, "Le poil de l'homme et des animaux" (The hair of man and animals). In one of the first cases involving the identification of hairs, Rosella Rousseau is persuaded to confess to the murder of Germaine Bichon.

Edmund Locard, successor to Alexandre Lacassagne as professor of forensic medicine at the University of Lyons, France, establishes the first police crime laboratory.

1913   Victor Balthazard, professor of forensic medicine at the Sorbonne, publishes the first article on individualizing bullet markings.

1915   The International Association for Criminal Identification, later the International Association of Identification (IAI), is organized in Oakland, California.

1920   U.S. Army officer Calvin Goddard, with forensic scientist Charles Waite, chemist Phillip O. Gravelle, and physicist John H. Fisher, perfects the comparison microscope for use in bullet comparison.

1923   In *Frye v. United States*, polygraph test results are ruled inadmissible. The federal ruling introduces the concept of general acceptance and states that polygraph testing does not meet that criterion.

1924   Los Angeles, California, chief of police August Vollmer implements the first U.S. police crime laboratory.

U.S. Attorney General Harlan Fiske Stone appoints a young lawyer, J. Edgar Hoover, to "clean house" at the supposedly corrupt FBI.

1926   The Sacco and Vanzetti case popularizes the use of the comparison microscope for bullet comparison.

1932   The FBI establishes its own forensic laboratory.

1937   Forensic scientist Paul Leland Kirk assumes leadership of the criminology program at the University of California, Berkeley. He will create a major in technical criminology in 1945.

1950   August Vollmer, chief of police of Berkeley, California, establishes the School of Criminology at the University of California, Berkeley. Kirk presides over the major of criminalistics within the school.

The American Academy of Forensic Science is formed in Chicago, Illinois. The group also begins publication of the *Journal of Forensic Science.*

1953   Paul Kirk publishes *Crime Investigation,* one of the first comprehensive texts to encompass foundational theories as well as laboratory methods.

1971   British scientist Brian Culliford publishes *The Examination and Typing of Bloodstains in the Crime Laboratory,* establishing protocols and standard methods for typing of protein and enzyme markers.

1975   The *Federal Rules of Evidence,* originally promulgated by the U.S. Supreme Court, are enacted as a congressional statute.

1977   The Fourier transform infrared spectrophotometer (FTIR) is adapted for use in the forensic laboratory.

The FBI introduces the Automated Fingerprint Identification System (AFIS) with the first digitized scans of fingerprints.

1983 Polymerase chain reaction (PCR) is first conceived by bio-chemist Kary Mullis. The first paper on the technique is not published for two years.

1984 British scientist Alec Jeffreys develops the first DNA profiling test. His findings will be published in *Nature* in 1985.

1986 In the first use of DNA to solve a crime, Alec Jeffreys uses DNA profiling to identify Colin Pitchfork as the murderer of two young girls in England.

1987 DNA profiling is introduced for the first time in a U.S. criminal court.

New York v. Castro is the first case challenging the admissibility of DNA. It begins a chain of events that will create a widespread call for accreditation and quality control of forensic methods.

1991 Walsh Automation Inc. (now Forensic Technology, Inc.) launches the Integrated Ballistics Identification System, or IBIS, for the automated comparison of fired bullets and cartridge cases. This system is subsequently developed in collaboration with the Bureau of Alcohol, Tobacco, and Firearms (ATF).

1992 The FBI sponsors development of DRUGFIRE, an automated imaging system to compare marks left on fired cartridge cases.

1993 In *Daubert, et al. v. Merrell Dow Parmaceuticals,* a U.S. federal court refines the standard for admission of scientific evidence.

1996 In *State of Tennessee v. Paul Ware,* mitochondrial DNA typing is first admitted in a U.S. court.

1998 The National DNA Indexing System (NDIS), enabling interstate sharing of DNA information to solve crimes, is initiated by the FBI.

1999 IBIS and DRUGFIRE are integrated by the FBI and ATF, creating the National Integrated Ballistics Identification Network (NIBIN).

United States v. Byron Mitchell is the first legal case where the admissibility of forensic fingerprints evidence is challenged. The defense contends that the state has failed to establish that forensic fingerprinting is scientifically valid, in part stating, "Is there a scientific basis for a fingerprint examiner to make an identification, of absolute certainty, from a small distorted latent fingerprint fragment?" The U.S. District Court for the Eastern District of Pennsylvania's decision is that the defense's motion to exclude fingerprint evidence is denied.

2001   On September 11, 19 terrorists hijack four commercial passengers in a coordinated attack on the United States. The hijackers crash American Airlines flight 11 and United Airlines flight 175 into the World Trade Center in New York City; American Airlines flight 77 into the Pentagon in Arlington County, Virginia and United Airlines flight 93, crashes in Somerset County, Pennsylvania, after passengers attempt to regain control of the plane. The resulting 2,993 deaths, including the hijackers', leads to the largest single forensic investigation in U.S. history. Fingerprints, dental identification, DNA, and other forensic methods are used to identify the victims.

2003   The Forensic Science Educational Program Accreditation Commission (FEPAC), a standing committee of the American Academy of Forensic Sciences (AAFS), awards accreditation to the pilot group of four forensic science educational programs.

2004   Brandon Mayfield, an American attorney living in Oregon, is erroneously linked to the 2004 Madrid train bombings. The FBI arrests Mayfield in connection with the Madrid attacks, but he is never charged. An FBI internal review in 2005 subsequently determines that the individualization of Mayfield was in error, and the latent print is ultimately identified with a different subject.

2007   The American Academy of Forensic Sciences creates a new section, Digital and Multimedia Forensics, reflecting the growing use of digital information as evidence.

The National Academies of Science issues a report on the status and needs of forensic science, recommending a number of changes to improve the scientific foundation and operation of the profession.

GLOSSARY

analysis   the breaking of a complex problem down into smaller, more manageable parts for purposes of examination. The aim is that solving these smaller parts will lead to a solution of the more complex problem. Analytical chemistry, for example, is the study of the chemical composition of natural and artificial materials. By studying the components of a material, a greater understanding of that and other materials is achieved.

ballistics   the science of mechanics that deals with the motion, behavior, and effects of projectiles. The forensic analysis of firearms and their effects is not ballistics—the analysts do not study the bullets while they are in flight! Yet some identify the forensic study of firearms as ballistics. Forensic firearms analysis involves analyzing firearms, ammunition, and toolmark evidence in order to establish whether a certain firearm or tool was used in the commission of a crime.

chromatography   the collective term for a family of laboratory techniques for the separation of mixtures. It involves passing a mixture dissolved in a "mobile phase" through a stationary phase, which separates the analyte (the material of interest) to be measured from other molecules in the mixture and allows it to be isolated.

controls   augmenters of integrity in experiments through the isolation of variables as dictated by the scientific method in order to make a conclusion about such variables. Without positive controls (those that are known to provide a known result) and negative controls (those that are known to provide no result), it is difficult to sort out the effects of a cause in an experiment.

criminalistics   coined from the German *kriminalistik* to describe the examination and comparison of biological evidence, trace evidence, impression evidence (such as fingerprints, footwear impressions, and tire tracks), controlled substances, ballistics (firearm examination), and other evidence in criminal investigations. Criminalistics is sometimes used in place of the term *forensic science.*

critical rationalism   philosophy holding that scientific theories, and any other claims to knowledge, can and should be criticized rationally and (if they have empirical content) can and should be subjected to tests that may falsify them. Those claims to knowledge that are potentially falsifiable can then be admitted to the body of empirical science. Further testing can lead to retention or rejection. If retained, further testing may be made based on criticism received and how severe such criticism has been. The longer a theory is retained, the stronger that theory is held.

direct transfer   the transfer of a material from one object to another by direct physical contact. Getting mud from your shoes onto the kitchen floor is direct transfer from the shoes to the floor. Direct transfer is part of the concept of the exchange principle described by Edmund Locard, a French forensic scientist.

DNA analysis   the analysis of deoxyribonucleic acid (DNA), also known as DNA typing or DNA profiling, a technique used to distinguish between individuals using samples of their DNA. Its invention by Dr. Alec Jeffreys at the University of Leicester was announced in 1984. Although two people will have the vast majority of their DNA sequence in common, DNA analysis exploits highly variable repeating sequences. It is possible to establish that a particular DNA profile is extremely unlikely to have arisen by coincidence, except in the case of identical twins, who will have identical genetic profiles. DNA analysis is used in forensic science to identify or exclude individuals potentially involved in criminal activities.

evidence   anything that supports or weakens an assertion. This can be physical evidence (a firearm), written documents (for example, a threatening letter), eyewitness testimony (a suspect leaving the residence), or any of a variety of forms. Evidence is used in investigations and in the courtroom; it is what is analyzed in a forensic laboratory.

focal length   a measure of how strongly an optical system converges (focuses) or diverges (diffuses) light. A system with a shorter focal length has greater optical power than one with a longer focal length.

forensic science the science of discovering and interpreting associations between people, places, and things potentially involved in criminal activities.

friction ridge a raised portion of the epidermis on the palmar (palm and fingers) or plantar (sole and toes) skin, consisting of one or more connected ridge units of friction ridge skin. Fingerprints are made up of friction ridges.

hypothesis either a suggested explanation for a phenomenon or a reasoned proposal suggesting a possible correlation between multiple phenomena. The scientific method requires that one can test a scientific hypothesis. Scientists generally base such hypotheses on previous observations or on extensions of scientific theories. Even though the words *hypothesis* and *theory* are often used synonymously, a scientific hypothesis is not the same as a scientific theory.

identification the act of placing something into a group with multiple members that share certain traits. All size-12 red-canvas tennis shoes would fall into the same group.

indirect transfer the transfer of a material from one object to another through an intermediary. Walking into the kitchen with muddy shoes is an indirect transfer of the mud from the ground outside to the floor inside using the shoes; the ground did not touch the floor itself. Indirect transfer is part of the exchange principle described by Edmund Locard, a French forensic scientist.

individualization the act of placing something into a group with only one member—that is, that thing is unique. Your size 12 red tennis shoes are unique, and no one else owns that pair.

infrared spectroscopy (also called IR spectroscopy) a spectroscopic method that deals with the infrared region of the electromagnetic spectrum (400–10 cm^{-1} or 1000–30 μm). It covers a range of techniques, the most common being a form of absorption spectroscopy. IR spectroscopy can be used to identify compounds or investigate sample composition.

laboratory (informally, lab) a facility that provides controlled conditions in which scientific research, experiments, and measurement may be performed.

lens an optical device with perfect or approximate axial symmetry that transmits and refracts light, concentrating or diverging the beam. A simple lens is a lens consisting of a single optical element. A compound lens is an array of simple lenses with a common axis; the use of multiple elements allows more optical aberrations to be corrected than is possible with a single element.

matter   commonly defined as the substance of which physical objects are composed. Matter constitutes much of the observable universe.

microscopy   the technique of using a microscope. Microscopy has evolved with the development of microscopes. Optical and electron microscopy involves the diffraction, reflection, or refraction of radiation (including visible light and electrons) incident upon the subject of study, and the subsequent collection of this scattered radiation in order to build up an image. The items to be studied are typically very small, and so lenses are used to increase the visibility of the samples.

mitochondrion   (plural, mitochondria) in cell biology, a membrane-enclosed organelle found in most eukaryotic cells. These organelles range from 1 to 10 micrometers (μm) in size. Mitochondria are sometimes described as "cellular power plants" because they generate most of the cell's energy supply.

Planck's constant   (denoted h) a physical constant that is used to describe the sizes of quanta. Named after Max Planck, one of the founders of quantum theory, it plays a central part in the theory of quantum mechanics. The Planck constant is used to describe quantization, a phenomenon occurring in subatomic particles, such as electrons and photons, in which certain physical properties occur in fixed amounts rather than assuming a continuous range of possible values.

refraction   the change in direction of a wave due to a change in its speed. This is most commonly seen when a wave passes from one medium to another. A drinking straw in a glass of water demonstrates refraction as it appears to split between the air and the water.

serology   the study of body fluids, especially blood, semen, saliva, and urine, for diagnostic or forensic purposes. Knowing your bloodtype is a result of a serological test.

spectroscopy   the study of the interaction between radiation and matter as a function of wavelength λ (lambda); any measurement of a quantity as a function of either wavelength or frequency.

testimony   a form of evidence that is obtained from a witness who makes a solemn statement or declaration of fact. Testimony may be oral or written, and it is usually made by oath or affirmation under penalty of lying (perjury). Unless a witness is testifying as an expert witness, testimony in the form of opinions or inferences is generally limited to those opinions or inferences that are rationally based on the perceptions of the witness and are helpful to a clear understanding of the witness's testimony. Experts may testify as to their opinions and interpretations.

theory   in science, a mathematical or logical explanation, or a testable model of the manner of interaction of a set of natural phenomena, capable of predicting future occurrences or observations of the same kind, and capable of being tested through experiment or otherwise falsified through empirical observation.

tool mark   any impression, cut, gouge, or abrasion caused by a tool or implement coming into contact with another object.

trace evidence   any evidence, because of its size or texture, that is readily transferred from one location to another. Hairs, fibers, paint, soil, and glass, among other materials, are considered forms of trace evidence.

ultraviolet light   (UV light) electromagnetic radiation with a wavelength shorter than that of visible light but longer than soft X-rays. It is so named because the spectrum consists of electromagnetic waves with frequencies higher than those that humans identify as the color violet (purple).

FURTHER READING

Ashbaugh, David R. *Quantitative-Qualitative Friction Ridge Analysis: An Introduction to Basic and Advanced Ridgeology.* Boca Raton, Fla.: CRC Press, 1999. This book examines the latest methods and techniques in ridgeology, the science of friction ridge identification, and every facet of the discipline, from the history of friction ridge identification and its earliest pioneers and researchers to the scientific basis and the various steps of the identification process.

Black, Bert. "Evolving Legal Standards for the Admissibility of Scientific Evidence." *Science* 239 (2002): 1,508–1,512. This article discusses the problems posed for scientifically untrained judges and lawyers in ensuring the scientific validity of scientific evidence. It cites recent cases that indicate the results when courts do not hold expert witnesses to the standards and criteria of their own disciplines.

Block, Eugene B. *Science vs. Crime: The Evolution of the Police Lab.* San Francisco: Cragmont Publications, 1979. This book discusses the laboratory and deductive techniques found to aid in crime detection. Block was a newspaper reporter in San Francisco and followed the "crime beat" for many years. Many cases are briefly reviewed in this book, and it offers an overview of how science is used to combat crime.

Bodziak, William J. *Footwear Impression Evidence: Detection, Recovery, and Examination.* 2nd ed. Boca Raton, Fla.: CRC Press, 2000. This book describes the methods used worldwide to recover and identify footwear impressions from the scene of a crime. In this new edition, everything, including the original twelve chapters, bibliography, appendix, etc., has been clarified, updated and expanded. This edition includes updated and new information on recovery procedures and materials such as lifting, photography and casting; chemical enhancement; updated information about footwear manufacturing; footwear sizing; and known impression techniques and materials.

Butler, John M. *Forensic DNA Typing: Biology and Technology Behind STR Markers.* 2nd ed. Boston: Academic Press, 2005. This comprehensive handbook helps forensic scientists gain a better understanding of short tandem repeat markers (STRs) and the procedures needed to properly analyze them, while also helping professionals in the law enforcement and legal communities comprehend the complexities of DNA profiling.

Champod, Christophe, Chris J. Lennard, Pierre Margot, and Milutin Stoilovic. *Fingerprints and Other Ridge Skin Impressions.* Boca Raton, Fla.: CRC Press, 2004. This book features the insight of a recognized team of authorities, including contributors from a key institution for forensic research. Chapters cover all aspects of the subject, including the formation of friction ridges on the skin, deposition of latent prints, detection and enhancement of such marks, recording of fingerprint evidence, and fingerprint identification itself.

Cole, Simon A. *Suspect Identities: A History of Fingerprinting and Criminal Identification.* Cambridge, Mass.: Harvard University Press, 2001. Cole's comprehensive first book investigates the tangled intersections of scientific identification and law enforcement.

Deadman, Harold. "The Importance of Trace Evidence." In *Trace Evidence Analysis: More Cases from Mute Witnesses,* edited by Max M. Houck, 123–164. San Diego: Elsevier Academic Press, 2004. Written by top practicing forensic scientists, this edited collection of cases explains in detail the detective and analytic work that goes into solving complex cases.

Douglas, John E., Ann W. Burgess, Allen G. Burgess, and Robert K. Ressler. *Crime Classification Manual: A Standard System for Investigating and Classifying Violent Crimes.* 2nd ed. New York: Jossey-Bass, 2006. This book classifies the critical characteristics of the perpetrators and victims of major crimes—murder, arson, sexual assault, and nonlethal acts—based on the motivation of the offender.

Farley, Mark A., and James J. Harrington, eds. *Forensic DNA Technology.* Chelsea, Mich.: Lewis Publishers, 1991. Examines the legal and scientific issues relating to the implementation of DNA print technology in both the crime laboratory and the courtroom. Chapters have been written by many of the country's leading experts and trace the underlying theory and historical development of this technology.

Fisher, Barry A. J. *Techniques of Crime Scene Investigation*. 7th ed. Boca Raton, Fla.: CRC Press, 2004. The latest edition of this book examines concepts, field-tested techniques and procedures, and technical information concerning crime scene investigation. It has been widely adopted by police academies, community colleges, and universities and is recommended for preparation for certification exams. Written in an easy-to-read style, this comprehensive text offers up-to-date technical expertise that the author has developed over many years in law enforcement. Includes checklists, case studies, and 16 pages of full-color illustrated photos.

Garner, Bryan A., ed. *Black's Law Dictionary*. 8th ed. St. Paul, Minn.: Thomson West Group, 2005. This premier legal reference resource has more than 43,000 definitions and almost 3,000 quotations.

Gerber, Samuel M., ed. *Chemistry and Crime: From Sherlock Holmes to Today's Courtroom*. Washington, D.C.: American Chemical Society, 1983. This book provides an illuminating view of forensic science in fact and fiction and underlines the relationship between detective fiction and the development of modern forensics.

Gerber, Samuel M., and Richard Saferstein, eds. *More Chemistry and Crime: From Marsh Arsenic Test to DNA Profile*. Washington, D.C.: American Chemical Society, 1997. This book covers forensic disciplines and techniques such as detection of arsenic, forensic toxicology, dust analysis, examination of arson evidence, and DNA typing.

Goff, M. Lee. *A Fly for the Prosecution: How Insect Evidence Helps Solve Crimes*. Cambridge, Mass.: Harvard University Press, 2000. This book reports unflinchingly on the development of this field as an important adjunct to traditional means of investigation.

Gould, Stephen Jay. *The Mismeasure of Man*. Rev. ed. New York: W.W. Norton, 2008. Gould's brilliant, funny, engaging prose dissects the motivations behind those who would judge intelligence, and hence worth, by cranial size, convolutions, or score on extremely narrow tests.

Gross, Alan G., Joseph Z. Harmon, and Michael S. Reidy. *Communicating Science: The Scientific Article from the 17th Century to the Present*. Oxford: Oxford University Press, 2002. This book describes the development of the scientific article from its modest beginnings to the global phenomenon that it has become today.

Houck, Max M., ed. *Mute Witnesses: Trace Evidence Analysis*. San Diego: Elsevier Academic Press, 2001. Each chapter in this book, written by some of the top practicing forensic scientists, explains in detail the detective and analytic work that goes into solving complex cases.

———. *Trace Evidence Analysis: More Cases from Mute Witnesses*. San Diego: Elsevier Academic Press, 2004. This volume continues and builds upon the tradition of its successful companion title, *Mute Witnesses*, in explaining the solutions of complex cases by top scientists.

Kind, Stuart, and Michael Overman. *Science Against Crime*. New York: Doubleday, 1972. This book is considered a landmark in the literature of science examination within the field of crime investigation.

Locard, Edmond. "The Analysis of Dust Traces." *American Journal of Police Science* 1 (1930): 276–298. An incisive paper that presents the history of research into dust traces.

Maltoni, Davide, Dario Maio, Anil K. Jain, and Salil Prabhakar. *Handbook of Fingerprint Recognition*. New York: Springer-Verlag, 2003. This handbook on automatic fingerprint recognition provides in-depth coverage of the most recent advances and practices.

Mason, Clyde W. ed. *Handbook of Chemical Microscopy*. 4th ed. Vol 1. New York: Wiley-Interscience, 1983. This is a volume devoted to the principles and use of microscopes and accessories, and to the physical methods for the study of chemical problems.

National Institute of Justice. "Forensic Sciences: Review of Status and Needs." Gaithersburg, Md.: National Institute of Standards and Technology, 1999. This important report from the U.S. Department of Justice on the proposed issues and obstacles to education and training of forensic scientists was updated in March 2006.

Ou, C., et al. "Molecular Epidemiology of HIV Transmission in a Dental Practice." *Science* 256 (1992): 1,165–1,171. Human immunodeficiency virus type 1 (HIV-1) transmission from infected patients to health care workers has been well documented, but transmission from an infected health care worker to a patient has not been reported. This landmark article discusses the identification of an acquired immunodeficiency syndrome (AIDS) patient who had no known risk factors for HIV infection but who had undergone an invasive procedure performed by a dentist with AIDS. Six other patients of the dentist were found to be HIV-infected. Molecular biologic studies were conducted to complement the epidemiologic investigation.

Rhodes, Henry T. F. *Alphonse Bertillon: Father of Scientific Detection.* New York: Greenwood Press, 1968.

Roberts, L. "Science in Court: A Clash of Cultures." *Science* 257 (1992): 732–736.

Ryland, Scott, and Max M. Houck. "Only Circumstantial Evidence." In *Mute Witnesses: Trace Evidence Analysis,* edited by Max M. Houck, 117–138. San Diego: Academic Press, 2001. This case review outlines the death investigation and subsequent forensic evidence in the kidnapping of a young girl in central Florida. The evidence included plastic bags, textile fibers, and human and animal hairs. The case emphasizes the strength of combining various types of trace evidence.

Schneck, William M. "Cereal Murder in Spokane." In *Trace Evidence Analysis: More Cases from Mute Witnesses,* edited by Max M. Houck, 165–190. San Diego: Academic Press, 2004. The death of a young boy hinges on the microscopical analysis of stomach contents, soil, metal turnings, building materials, paint, and soot. Particles of food from breakfast cereal were identified in the vomit of the boy and linked to the boy's home environment. It is believed the father, who later committed suicide in jail, killed his son and set fire to the house for insurance.

The Science of Fingerprints. Washington, D.C.: Federal Bureau of Investigation, Government Printing Office, 1985. This publication is intended for law-enforcement officers and agencies to serve as a general reference on classification and fingerprint identification.

Shafer, Robert J., et al. eds. *A Guide to Historical Method.* 3rd ed. Homewood, Ill.: Dorsey Press, 1980. In this classic book on the method of historical research and inquiries, Shafer lays out the basic philosophies that support history as a discipline and historical research in particular. This is an excellent foundation for any student of history or other historical studies.

Taylor, Karen T. *Forensic Art and Illustration.* Boca Raton, Fla.: CRC Press, 2001. This book offers readers the benefit of Taylor's extensive knowledge and experience. It is the first book to provide complete coverage of all aspects of the field, and it includes much previously unavailable information.

Thomas, Ronald R. *Detective Fiction and the Rise of Forensic Science.* Cambridge: Cambridge University Press, 1999. This is the first book about the relationship between the development of forensic science in the 19th century and the new literary genre of detective fiction in Britain and America. Thomas is especially concerned with the authority the literary detective manages to secure through "devices"—fingerprinting, photography, lie detectors—and the ways in which those devices relate to broader questions of cultural authority at decisive moments in the history of the genre.

Thorwald, Jürgen. *The Century of the Detective,* translated by Richard and Clara Winston. New York: Harcourt, Brace & World, 1965. This is a fine source of famous cases told in greater detail than in most other sources.

———. *Crime and Science: The New Frontier in Criminology,* translated by Richard and Clara Winston. New York: Harcourt, Brace & World, 1967. Chapters in this early book on the science of forensics include many famous cases that were solved using newly discovered scientific techniques.

Tridico, Silvana R. "Hair of the Dog." In *Trace Evidence Analysis: More Cases from Mute Witnesses,* edited by Max M. Houck, 27–52. San Diego: Academic Press, 2004. This chapter reviews a case of dog hairs linking a suspect to the victim of a brutal murder in Australia. Research into identifying dog and cat hairs is included in the article, which also reviews the investigation of the case in detail.

Ubelaker, Douglas, and Henry Scammell. *Bones: A Forensic Detective's Casebook.* New York: HarperPaperbacks, 2000. This book explains how those in the field work with police to solve mysteries lacking clues except for a few bones, on the basis of which experts can determine a victim's race, age, and sex and often the cause of his or her death.

Waggoner, Kim. "The FBI Laboratory: 75 Years of Forensic Science Service." *Forensic Science Communications* 9, no. 4 (2007). An interesting essay on the history of this important bureau. Available online. URL:

http://www.fbi.gov/hq/lab/fsc/backissu/oct2007/research/2007_10_research01_test1.html. Accessed May 1, 2008.

Wheeler, Barbara. "Who Do You Believe?" In *Trace Evidence Analysis: More Cases from Mute Witnesses,* edited by Max M. Houck, San Diego: Academic Press, 2004. Trace evidence is used to sort fact from fiction in the investigation of an automobile accident. A witness said that the driver and passenger were both the same age, size, and wearing the same clothes, making it hard to sort out who was the driver and, therefore, at fault. Microscopic analysis of the clothing, shoes, and interior of the vehicle clearly indicated where both of the occupants of the vehicle were at the time of the crash.

Web Sites: Organizations in Forensic Science

Note: Many of the organizations listed below meet each year, sometimes multiple times, around the United States. Many have student membership status, and all of them provide additional information about their areas of interest on their Web sites.

American Academy of Forensic Sciences (AAFS). Available online. URL: www.aafs.org. Downloaded January 15, 2008. The AAFS is a nonprofit professional society organized in 1948 that is devoted to the improvement, administration, and achievement of justice through the application of science to the processes of law.

American Society of Crime Laboratory Directors (ASCLD). Available online. URL: www.ascld.org. Downloaded January 17, 2008. The ASCLD is a nonprofit professional society of crime laboratory directors and forensic science managers dedicated to promoting excellence in forensic science through leadership and innovation.

Association of Forensic Quality Assurance Managers (AFQAM). Available online. URL: www.afqam.org. Downloaded January 17, 2008. The AFQAM promotes standardized practices and professionalism in quality assurance management for the forensic community.

California Association of Criminalists (CAC). Available online. URL: www.cacnews.org. Downloaded January 17, 2008. The CAC recognizes and promotes achievements in criminalistics.

International Association for Identification (IAI). Available online. URL: www.theiai.org. Downloaded January 17, 2008. The IAI is committed to six objectives: to associate persons in the forensic science profession; to keep them up to date and informed; to advance the relevant sciences; to encourage research; to provide training and education; and to promote the dissemination of this information through its publications, thereby fostering a relationship among forensic practitioners worldwide.

Mid-Atlantic Association of Forensic Sciences (MAAFS). Available online. URL: www.maafs.org. Downloaded January 17, 2008. The mission of the MAAFS is to encourage the exchange and dissemination of ideas and information within the fields of recognized forensic sciences through improving contacts between persons and laboratories engaged in the forensic sciences, to stimulate research and the development of new and/or improved techniques, and to promote high standards of performance and facilitate professional acknowledgment of persons working in recognized forensic science disciplines.

Midwest Association of Forensic Scientists (MAFS). Available online. URL: www.mafs.net. Downloaded January 17, 2008. The purpose of the MAFS is to encourage the exchange of ideas and information within the forensic sciences by improving contacts between people and laboratories engaged in forensic science. The association supports and stimulates research and development of new and/or improved techniques, and it works to promote the improvement of professional expertise of persons working in the field of forensic science through education, scientific seminars, and research grants.

National Association of Medical Examiners (NAME). Available online. URL: www.thename.org. Downloaded January 17, 2008. NAME is a national professional organization of medical examiners, death investigators, and death investigation system administrators involved in the medico-legal investigation of deaths of public interest in the United States. The association was founded in 1966 with the dual purposes of fostering the professional growth of medical death investigators and disseminating the professional and technical information vital to the continuing improvement of the medical investigation of violent, suspicious, and unusual deaths.

Northeastern Association of Forensic Scientists (NEAFS). Available online. URL: www.neafs.org. Downloaded January 17, 2008. The

NEAFS is a nonprofit regional organization of forensic scientists. Its stated purposes are to exchange ideas and information within the field of forensic science; to foster friendship and cooperation among the various laboratory personnel; to encourage a high level of competency among professionals in the field of forensic science; to promote recognition of forensic science as an important component of the criminal justice system; to stimulate increased implementation of existing techniques, along with research and development of new techniques within the field; and to encourage financial support for these efforts.

Northwestern Association of Forensic Scientists (NWAFS). Available online. URL: www.nwafs.org. Downloaded January 17, 2008. The NWAFS is a nonprofit organization that was formed to encourage the dissemination of information within the field of forensic science and discuss problems of common interest, to foster friendship and cooperation among forensic scientists, and to stimulate research and development of new techniques within the field.

Society of Forensic Toxicologists, Inc. (SOFT). Available online. URL: www.soft-tox.org. Downloaded January 26, 2008. SOFT is an organization composed of practicing forensic toxicologists and those interested in the discipline for the purpose of promoting and developing forensic toxicology.

Southern Association of Forensic Scientists (SAFS). Available online. URL: www.southernforensic.org. Downloaded January 26, 2008. The objectives of the SAFS are to encourage the dissemination of information within the field of forensic sciences and discuss problems of common interest, to foster friendship and cooperation among forensic scientists, to stimulate research and development of new techniques within the field, to promote the use of standardized methodology and presentation of conclusions; to encourage compilation of statistical data of value in the field, to assist in maintaining a high level of professional competence among practicing forensic scientists, and to lend assistance to law enforcement planning agencies and to colleges and universities in the development of forensic science and related curricula.

Southwestern Association of Forensic Scientists (SWAFS). Available online. URL: www.swafs.us. Downloaded January 26, 2008. SWAFS is a nonprofit organization that was formed to provide an association for persons who are actively engaged in the profession of scientific examination of physical evidence in an organized body so that the profession of all its disciplines may be effectively and scientifically practiced. SWAFS also seeks to exchange information among forensic scientists in order to improve techniques, to encourage research in forensic science, and to keep its members apprised of the latest techniques and discoveries in forensic science.

INDEX

Italic page numbers indicate illustrations.